# The Journey of the
# Terminally Ill

# The Journey of the Terminally Ill

◆

## Through the Eyes and Heart of a Hospice Nurse

*Erin McGraw, RN BSN*

iUniverse, Inc.

New York  Lincoln  Shanghai

# The Journey of the Terminally Ill
## Through the Eyes and Heart of a Hospice Nurse

iUniverse, Inc.

For information address:
iUniverse, Inc.
2021 Pine Lake Road, Suite 100
Lincoln, NE 68512
www.iuniverse.com

ISBN: 0-595-31464-3

Printed in the United States of America

Dedicated to all those who have
Faced their terminal illness and death
With incredible strength and courage
And all their loved ones who stayed by their side
Loving them and caring for them until the last breath was taken

# Contents

# *Acknowledgements*

I would like to thank Alys and Marty for all your help, patience, and mentoring. I couldn't have done this without you. Thank-you to all my family and friends who have been so supportive and excited about this adventure that I decided to take on. Thank-you Joanna for taking a chance on someone without hospice experience and hiring me, and to all the wonderful hospice nurses who trained me and taught me what hospice was all about. I am grateful to all the different hospice team members for their support through those difficult times. Thank-you Oprah for the inspiration to write this book, and thank-you to all the patients and their families and friends whom have allowed me into your homes and lives during such a difficult time. I admire you all; you are the true heroes in my eyes.

# Introduction

This book deals with a subject most people try to avoid talking about, death. It tells the stories of terminally ill patients, how they deal with what is happening to them, and what is going to happen. It tells of the physical changes within the body as the disease progresses, and also what goes on emotionally with the patient and their loved ones. It is told through the eyes of a hospice nurse, and what she experiences taking care of the terminally ill on a daily basis.

The book tells of hospice, what it is, and how it helps these patients and their loved ones through the most difficult and frightening time of their lives. I hope it helps you realize that there is support and help out there and that there are professional hospice staff who take pride in their work. They have the knowledge of how to care for the dying and their families.

The stories in this book are based on patients and their loved ones who have touched my heart. There are so many others stories and patients I have cared for who were no less important. The stories I wrote about were the ones that had the biggest impact on me. They have made me a better hospice nurse and a better person. The lessons I learned from each one are different, as was the impact they had on me. I hope that you will be able to let each story affect you in your own special way, and draw similar lessons or lessons all your own from the lives lived, lost and the ones left behind.

The first story is of a hospice patient that takes place shortly after I started working in a hospice facility, while I still had no real experience about death and dying. With each experience, my confidence and capability grew as a hospice nurse and I was able to handle the more challenging situations with ease. As you will see, though, no matter how long you do hospice work your emotions still overcome you at times. We are all human, and all feel the pain of heartache as someone we love dies. The last story was a real honor for me to be able to follow someone so special and incredible on her journey.

My hope is that someone will draw courage and strength from these stories knowing they are not alone, and that the book may inspire others to seek out work or volunteer opportunities at a hospice or specialize in hospice nursing. It is a truly rewarding job and the dying teach you so much about life and what is important. Some patients are alone and need a kind ear to listen to them, touch them, and make them feel like they still matter even though they may be gone tomorrow or next week. The families and loved ones who helplessly stand by and watch their loved one die also need kindness and support. You need to know that you are not alone and hospice is there for you too. There is as much support as is needed for anyone who reaches out, and there is always a hug or the gentle touch of a hand when you don't know if you can go on or don't know what to do.

Even though death may be weeks or months away, patients with terminal conditions still have so much life to live, and hospice helps them live as much as possible and as comfortably as possible for as long as they can. There are still memories to be made, laughter to experience, places to go, people to see, and reminiscing to do. Every day when I look into my patient's eyes I see a life lived, stories needing to be told, and lessons that need to be taught. Dying is a journey that everyone must go through, just like living is.

# *John's Story*

Sometimes I wonder what led me to hospice nursing and why it is my calling. Life experiences sometimes have a bigger impact on us than we realize at the time. The experiences that bring us the most pain can often turn out to be positive later. Writing this book made me realize that my first death experience might be what led me to love hospice work so much, and why I have always wanted to work with cancer patients. Maybe, in some way, my friend guided me to where I am today.

My first experience with death was back in high school when I was just sixteen years old. My high school was in a small town and consisted of only about three hundred students. Everyone knew everyone, and even though there were the usual high school "cliques," everyone got along pretty well and respected each other. My particular "clique" consisted of about ten to fifteen people at any given time. We were a pretty close group of friends. Some of us had been friends since elementary school and some of us had just become friends in high school. We were together all the time. We would always talk between classes and sometimes even during class, getting us into trouble. Almost every Friday night, and sometimes Saturday nights too, we would all hang out at someone's house and watch movies or go out to eat. It was as if we couldn't live without each other. There was not much to do in a small town, but we always seemed to find our own fun and laugh a lot. Of course, since we were so close there were times we got sick of each other and would occasionally have petty little high school fights, which seemed like the end of the world at the time. Someone would not be talking to someone for some reason or another and half the time didn't even know why. When this happened it would usually split the group into taking sides, which caused tension among everyone. Fortunately, the fights never lasted very long, and before we knew it everyone would be talking again. What made our friendships truly special is that we were always there for one another through the tough times and all the usual traumas of being teenagers. We went through parents splitting up, lots of broken hearts, broken friendships, bad grades, challenging classes, and the ever-changing self-esteem issues of growing up. I feel very lucky to have had such wonderful friends, and blessed to still keep in touch with some of them. Little did we know that the deep bond of our friendships would soon be put to the test and changed forever by a very grown-up and serious situation involving one of our friends.

It all started at the beginning of my junior year of high school. We were all blissfully unaware of the path it would take, and how it would change our lives. We were all over at a friend's house having a get-together. There were people everywhere. A small group of us decided to sit in the hot tub. I was sitting across from my friend John. We were all just talking about the usual gossip stuff high school kid's talk about; who was going with whom and the latest rumors floating around. We were laughing and having a good time, with not a care in the world. John mentioned how good the hot water felt on his back. I asked him what he did to his back and he said he didn't know but that it had been hurting him for about a week or so and was getting worse. He brushed it off as nothing and said that if it got any worse he would go see a doctor. So, we went about laughing and joking around like the conversation had never taken place. It was never mentioned again and the party eventually ended later that night. The next morning I got a phone call from one of my friends, John's girlfriend at the time, who told me that later that night on the way home from the party John doubled over in pain and ended up being taken to the hospital. They assessed him and determined it was probably appendicitis. They took him into surgery and removed his appendix. After getting home from the hospital it didn't take John long to get back to his old self. Soon it was like nothing ever happened except for when he would show us his scar, thinking that it was a battle wound or something. We all returned to the carefree, immortal world of being teenagers. Within the next month, John started missing school a lot, which was unusual for him but no one thought anything of it. It didn't take long for the word to get out that he was back in the hospital with back pain again. His best friend, who was part of our group of friends, kept in contact with John's parents and by word of mouth we were all assured that everything was fine. He was released in a couple of days and he told us that the doctors found a spot on one of his kidneys. The doctors didn't think it was anything to worry about at this time and decided to "just watch it." Although I was not a nurse yet, but knew that I wanted to be, I found it a little odd that they just wanted to "watch it," but I kept my thoughts to myself. Of course, we didn't get any more information than that because John didn't like dwelling on it. He was too busy wanting to go out and have fun. He always had endless amounts of energy so he was always on the go. He had an amazing attitude, spirit, and a great sense of humor. He always had everyone laughing, although he never thought he was that funny.

I kept thinking, "He is fifteen years old, this couldn't be anything serious, could it?" Nothing serious could ever happen to us. But John was not getting better, his parents decided to switch doctors and hospitals. Shortly after that he found himself having surgery to remove the "spot" that was now almost the size of his kidney, whereas before it was the size of a golf ball. We all got the news after the last school bell rang. Some of us decided to pile into a car and drive two hours to go see him in the hospital. All the way down there, there was talking and laughing, just like it was another trip to the big city. Not until we pulled up to the hospital did we remember the purpose of the trip. Our friend was in the hospital, and this was the first serious, grown-up thing that had happened to someone in our tight group of friends. Everyone became very quiet as we pulled into a parking spot and we walked into the hospital in complete silence. Walking around in the hospital was pretty scary for me, because it was my first time in a hospital and I knew that being in the hospital and having surgery was serious business. We all paused at the doorway of his room, not wanting to go in and not sure what we would find on the other side, but we knew we needed to be there for him. We all cautiously walked into his room as a group and immediately started laughing because John was sitting up in his bed with an exam glove pulled over his head. He was blowing the gloves up like balloons. Of course, it didn't take long before all the guys joined in and had exam gloves on their heads too. Even though John tried his hardest not to laugh because it hurt, he ended up laughing anyway. Between fits of laughter, I breathed a sigh of relief. "Everything is going to be ok now," I thought to myself, wondering what was going through everyone else's minds. We just didn't share our feelings about what was going on. We talked about everything else but that. We couldn't stay long because it was a school night and by this time John was exhausted, so we started on our long journey home. The car was pretty quiet all the way back except for an occasional, "He'll be ok." I wanted to share everyone else's belief but I remember feeling that something was not right, that John was not being told everything, and we weren't either. Just about the time everything started getting back to normal, the news came. The diagnosis hit us like a brick wall. The word came when we were in school. John's mom had called school to tell his best friend and to have him tell all of us. It was cancer. None of us knew what to say. We just stared at his best friend as if to say, "You're kidding, right?" Aware that his friend was known for pulling jokes on people, we all hoped this was just another one of his jokes. If it were, it wouldn't have been a funny one. But as each of us took the time to look at his face and look into his eyes, we realized this was no joke. I remember my body going completely numb. I felt like I was floating. I couldn't move. I just stood there thinking, "Cancer, it can't be cancer, he is fifteen years old, he is one of us." Even though we were in the middle of the busy hallway between classes, I heard nothing and saw nothing. I knew it, all those feelings I had been having about something else going on were right, but I didn't want them to be right. Why couldn't they have been wrong? I remember having dinner with my family that night, and not really knowing what to say to them, thinking for some reason that they would not understand. I didn't know anything about cancer and actually remember thinking "Is it contagious?" "How did he get it?" "What does it feel like?" "Is he going to die?" I had so many questions, and although I had the best family and friends in the world, I felt so alone. I felt like I could talk to no one because I didn't know anyone who had ever known anyone with cancer. It was like a bad word; no one ever talked about "cancer." I was holding back my tears that night, not sure whether I should cry or not. I had no idea what to feel or what to do. "How could this be happening?" I thought to myself.

The next morning I woke up thinking that it was a dream, but when I got to school and looked into everyone's bloodshot, swollen eyes, I knew it wasn't. We didn't even know what to say to each other. We knew how to support each other through broken hearts and "teenage stuff," but not cancer. Cancer was something for grown-ups to deal with. As soon as they learned that it was cancer, John went back into surgery to remove the whole kidney to make sure they "got it all." The doctors and John's parents were optimistic that it was all gone. I wanted to be optimistic, and I really tried to be but was never really convinced they got it all. I always had a feeling in my gut that John was not going to be ok, but I knew I could tell no one. I didn't even know that someone could live with just one kidney at the time. John was pretty withdrawn for a while, recovering from the surgery and being alone with his thoughts. He never liked anyone to see him down. After recovering from his surgery, John started chemotherapy. This was all happening around Christmas time and John just loved Christmas. He was so upset because he could not snowmobile, which he loved to do, or go outside because the air was too cold and his immune system was down. Although he was pretty weak, he would never admit it. He never admitted being in pain either. His house became our hangout. We would all go over there and talk, watch movies, and play games. Although we all wanted things back to normal, we knew that they weren't. We tried so hard to act "normal" around John, but it was very difficult because it was so physically obvious that he was sick. In the back of my mind I wondered if things would ever be the same, if John would ever be the same. Even through the laughter, everyone's hearts were heavy with worry, uncertainty, and fear especially mine I think. John's mom became extremely protective of him and worried about every little sniffle. She would only allow us to stay for a short time. Of course, John played everything off like it was nothing, and that his mom was overreacting. He always felt like he had to remain so strong and never wanted to show any weakness to anyone. Chemotherapy had made him completely bald, and he always tied a bandana around his head. He would show us a flash of his baldhead, but it made him uncomfortable to show even us. He was never very big so when he lost weight he became extremely thin. The chemotherapy treatments left him pretty sick. At the beginning he started off so strong and was handling all the side effects with such courage. He would say, "I can do this," and "I am going to beat this thing." But halfway through, I remember talking to him one day and he told me how incredibly thirsty he was but couldn't even keep water down. I could tell that he was getting pretty discouraged about the whole thing. "I am tired of being sick, I just want to eat and drink like a normal person without the fear of throwing everything up as soon as I swallow it," he said. He tried so long and so hard to be brave, but I could tell that with each chemotherapy treatment his courage and strength were diminishing, along with his physical health. John endured chemotherapy for six months or so. We didn't see much of him during that time because he was hardly ever in school and he was so sick he wasn't up for company. His mom limited the amount of people contact he had because of his decreased immune system. He finally made it through his last chemotherapy treatment. He did it! But he remained weak and very thin for months afterwards.

After his chemotherapy ended and the doctors declared him "in remission". That is when we all noticed a change in his personality. He started isolating himself and pushing us away. He didn't want anything to do with us anymore. He had found a new group of friends to hang out with. He did stay close to his two best friends, but he treated the rest of us like we were acquaintances. Of course, this made all of us very confused, angry, and hurt. I kept in touch with his mother and her best friend who was also my boss. His mom explained to me that we all reminded John of being sick. She tried reassuring all of us that we still meant a lot to him and always would. Well, at the time that was little comfort for the hurt and confusion we were all feeling. John felt like he had put us all through enough and wanted a clean slate now that he was well. My boss also tried to explain that if John were to get sick again he wouldn't want all of us to go through it all again. She was a great comfort and support to me, and it was nice to hear an adult's perspective on everything. It all makes sense now as I am sitting here as an adult, but as a teenager you just feel the pain of losing a friend and never really understanding why. We were such a tight group of friends it was hard to imagine how quickly we had been replaced. John did not allow himself to get too close to anyone after that. It was all his way of dealing with whatever he was going through then, and had gone through. No matter how hurt we felt, we knew we needed to respect his feelings.

Even though we no longer hung out with him, we still considered him our friend and would have been there for him in a second if he needed us. He started to get back to going to school, and for some time he seemed to be getting well. He would say "hi" to us in passing in the hallways, but that is all we got. We hoped and believed it was behind him, that he could finally go back to being a carefree teenager. I was happy for him but I couldn't help but wonder how he really was because he still looked so sick to me. I still had that little voice inside me telling me that things were not all right. A few times I noticed that he would be walking stiffly, and bent forward a little. I would ask him if he was ok and he always said yes. He had a permanent grimace on his face from the pain but he was not about to admit anything to anyone. I tried reaching out to him but got nowhere. How alone and scared he must have felt, but he continued to carry on in true "John fashion," never wanting anyone to see him weak or appear that he needed someone. I can imagine him saying to himself, "I must remain strong."

It was now the second semester of my senior year and John's junior year. It was obvious to everyone that he was sick again. Some days I would see him walking down the halls bent over in pain and barely able to get up from the desk. I can't imagine how much pain he was in and how he could possibly go on like this. Every morning I would wake up and wonder "Will this be the day that he dies?" It was like a big bomb sitting right in front of us. We all knew it was going to explode but didn't know when. I kept hoping, "Please just make it until graduation." There was a bunch of us out of the group, including his two best friends, who would be graduating, and we all wanted him to see us graduate. Whether we were close friends or not, he always held a special place in all our hearts because of what we had been through together. About five months or so after his last chemotherapy treatment, word spread once again that John was sick. He had been having severe back pain and trouble breathing for some time but did not want anyone to know. He said he never wanted to be put on life-support and did not want to go through any more chemotherapy or surgeries. Of course, he was afraid that his parents had other ideas, so he waited until he almost collapsed and could hardly breathe. His parents rushed him down to the hospital where they got the news that the cancer was back and had spread. John was going to have to be put on a respirator to help him breathe. He refused. Now John's parents were faced with the most difficult and painful decision of their lives. Do they honor their son's wishes and let him go, or do everything to fight for his life? With very heavy hearts, John's parents decided to honor his wishes and refuse any extraordinary measures to keep him alive. John had expressed that he wanted to die at home, so his parents carried his frail body out of the hospital and drove him home. His parents had a beautiful home with a big bay window overlooking the lake—his favorite place in the world. John told them that he wanted to die looking out over the lake, so his parents set up a bed in the living room facing the lake. Less than twenty-four hours later, in the early hours of a February morning, at the age of seventeen, John passed away peacefully in his home. His parents said he was looking out at the lake, just as he wanted.

I was sitting in social studies class, trying to pay attention, when the school counselor knocked on the door. I didn't think anything of it until he started naming off all of John's friends to come out into the hallway. As I followed the others out into the hallway I saw that he had already gathered together a few of us. That's when my heart stopped and I knew before he even said the words. Then he said the words that I never thought I would hear and I didn't want to hear, "John passed away early this morning in his home." The statement was difficult to understand because everything was such a blur and it sounded all mumbled and like an echo. We all just stood there like stone statues; there were no tears or words exchanged. I remember thinking to myself that I was glad he got to die the way he wanted to and that he was no longer in pain, but I said nothing. It was as if I didn't have a voice. We all moved mechanically down the hallway to notify the last of our group of friends. Then we were all lead into the counseling office to "talk about it." I remember everyone looking at each other and having an unspoken understanding that we did not want to sit there and "talk about it." We just wanted to be alone with each other, just us because we felt we were the only ones who understood. We had to get out of the building. I remember feeling trapped, I couldn't breathe, I had to get out, go somewhere, anywhere, and somehow outrun and change what had just happened. The counselor said that if we could get permission from our parents we were excused from school. One by one, like robots, we called our parents and one by one each of us got permission to leave. I remember calling my mom at home and there was no answer. Panic went through me. "What if I have to stay here alone without my friends? I can't stay here! I have to be with my friends!" Then I called my dad at work and told him what had happened and asked if I could leave school. He reluctantly agreed. As soon as we were all cleared, we agreed to meet at a friend's house who didn't live too far away. We went over there and talked, cried, and stared at each other, wishing that somehow this was all a dream. I really don't remember much of that day, it was all so fuzzy, my body felt so heavy, and I was so exhausted. It felt so good to be among my friends though. I felt that they were the only ones in the world who understood. It hurt all of us that we did not get to say good-bye to him, but somehow knew that we meant a lot to him up to the very end. Even though the house was filled with people I was alone with my thoughts, in my own uncertain foggy world. Friends were not supposed to die of cancer before graduating from high school. Things like this didn't happen in our small town.

The next day school was optional, so we all decided not to go and we gathered at another friend's house. Everyone knowing and dreading what we would have to face in the next few days—John's funeral. Until then, to some extent we could still be in denial. A small group of us found ourselves in an upstairs bedroom. We were not talking. We just listened to two songs over and over, "Everybody Wants to go to Heaven" and "The Rose." We listened to these songs for hours, the whole time just staring at the floor, sometimes glancing up at each other and letting the tears fall down our cheeks, then back to the floor. There were no words to describe what we all felt; even all the tears did not fully describe our pain. I never knew your heart could physically hurt so much. That night, after crying and listening to the music all day, we threw a party in John's honor. Even though we were all completely exhausted, it felt good to celebrate his life instead of the constant mourning of his death. He would not have wanted us to mourn him anyway. It was a relief to laugh and talk to friends again, to hug each other and reminisce about the times we had together and to be thankful John was no longer in pain. I felt less like a zombie and more human again.

The day of his funeral finally arrived—the day we didn't ever want to come. It brought everything home for me. There was no more denying that this was a dream. We all walked into the church together, holding hands. We followed each other like a train of zombies. We found our seats and sat down, never once letting go of one another. This was all very real, and seeing his coffin being brought in the church finally made me realize that this had really happened. John was dead. Our friend was gone. I felt pain I never knew existed, and I am glad that I had the support of my friends around me. We held each other up and supported one another knowing that we were all going through the same loss. It was the only comforting thing at such a confusing, painful time. I don't remember much about the service, it was all such a blur, and all I could do was stare at his coffin trying to comprehend that John was in there. As people starting filing out of the church, other students, some I didn't even know that well, came up to me and hugged me, offering their condolences. I knew they were hugging me but really couldn't feel their arms around me; I was numb. We decided to stay behind after everyone left the church. No one wanted to go to the cemetery. We stayed inside the church looking at all the pictures and flower arrangements, and talking, crying, and just holding one another, not wanting to ever let go of each other. The world without each other was now a scary place. We had barely left each other's sides since the day he died. We had all been there from the very beginning and now found ourselves at the end not really knowing what to do or how we would go on from here. In a strange way we thought that if we let go something might happen to someone else. Our world was no longer innocent and immortal.

We finally decided to leave the church and meet at a friend's house and have another party in John's honor. We didn't know what else to do, and it helped dull the pain. We also wanted John to be looking down at us celebrating his life and moving on, not sitting around mourning him. He would want to see us laughing again; living. After the party no one talked about John for a long time. I know that he was on everyone's minds but his name was not mentioned. Most of us were busy getting ready for graduation. This was the first time in a long time that everyone was happy and acting like normal teenagers again. John's death was getting easier to cope with and we began to talk about him in a cheerful way, remembering things we had done with him. We then came up with an idea to hold a memorial dance to raise money for some kind of memorial. John's mother thought it was a wonderful idea and said that John would have been very proud to have such good friends. The dance was a bigger success than we could have ever expected. We raised around eight hundred dollars or more. This was something we all felt we needed to do to fully move on. A couple of us and a good friend of John's mom decided to present the money along with a poem I wrote and a card signed by all of us to John's mom at his gravesite. She graciously accepted, then immediately burst into tears and ran off down a dirt road. I started to cry, too, because I had never seen someone in so much emotional pain before. I could tell that her heart was broken in a thousand pieces and I could do nothing about it. My heart ached for her and I felt so guilty for making her cry; for bringing her so much pain. I remember looking down at John's grave thinking, "I'm so sorry." I was beginning to think what a big mistake I had made. I should have never given the money to her there. I wished I would have mailed it or given it to her friend, so I would not have to see all her pain. Her friend, with whom I was fairly close, was right by my side and tried to assure me that I had done nothing wrong. Even as we walked away she still did not have me convinced. I just couldn't say "sorry" enough to both John and his mom. John's mom eventually calmed down, gave me a hug, and thanked me through all her tears and pain. "John would be so proud of you guys, he was so lucky to have such wonderful friends," she said. "I know he is here watching us and he knows what you guys did and that is why I felt this would be an appropriate place." After she said that I felt a little better. With the money we raised they built a wooden gazebo right by the lake. Next to the gazebo is a rock with a plaque on it with a saying and his picture. Every summer we all try to visit the gazebo, either together or alone, to make sure we never forget our friend. The poem "Roads" is something I wrote shortly after John's death, expresses the journey he took alone and the journey we took together.

# *Roads*

It has been such a long hard road
A road filled with uncertainty, and fear
A road you traveled with such courage and strength
Now the road has finally ended,
Along with all the pain
And suffering

This road was rough and painful
Traveled only by you,
Everyone else just followed
Never knowing exactly what you were going through
But we continued to be right behind you, holding you up
And even when you pushed us away
We continued to see you through it in spirit
Knowing we would all meet again at the end

The end of this road is filled with sadness
It hurt us to see you suffer
And it hurts us because you are gone,
But there is a certain kind of peace,
Even though no one knows where you have gone
Or what it is like there
We know that you are no longer suffering
And are at peace

We all stood there at the end of the road
Knowing you were no longer physically with us
So we silently stood to say our good-byes,
Stood and stared,
Wondering,
Why you had to be taken from us

Then all of us wiped our tears
Turned around and headed back
Back down the road of life
Walking hand in hand
Knowing that we must continue on
Without you


Even though our lives took different roads
And yours ended too soon
There is comfort that you will watch over us
And keep us safe.

# The Beginning

I did not set out to be a hospice nurse. I knew that it was one of my interests but wasn't sure why, because in nursing school we were not taught about hospice. We got to spend one day with a hospice nurse and that was the extent of it. I knew what hospice was but that was about it. I knew I liked home care, but after graduating it was all so overwhelming I wasn't sure which way to go. It took me two months to find a job; no one wanted to hire a new graduate, especially in home care. Everyone would always tell me, "Go get some hospital experience first." But the hospital didn't want anyone without hospital experiences either. I don't know where everyone expected new graduates to get hospital experience. Well, after getting nowhere with home care I was offered a night position in a hospital. I was not thrilled about it but knew that I better take it, because someone was finally willing to give me a chance without having experience. I worked on a very busy medical-surgical floor and did twelve-hour night shifts. I did learn a lot but I knew that my heart was not in it. It was very stressful and I never really liked it. I had barely made it to the six-month mark when I knew it was time to look for something else. Then, out of the blue, I got a call from one of my classmates who remembered that I mentioned a couple times that I might like to try hospice. She was currently working at a hospice facility and was quitting to go get hospital experience. So I went down and applied and they hired me. I wasn't totally sure about it, and actually didn't think it through at all because all I could think was "I don't have to work in the hospital anymore."

I walked in my first day, a little nervous of course. Everyone who worked there greeted me with open arms and they were so friendly, which put me at ease right away. Everyone was so excited to have me, and didn't care that I had no experience. The facility was nice and clean and had a cozy, homelike atmosphere to it. It was pretty small, which I liked. I felt very comfortable and welcomed there. All the nurses seemed happy in their jobs and most had been there for a long time. I was amazed at how much the staff and even some of the patients were laughing and smiling. I always thought a hospice would be dark, depressing, and quiet. But it was just the opposite; it was a place filled with laughter and life. The nurses were constantly telling jokes and laughing among the patients, their families, and other staff members. It looked like such a wonderful, fun place to work. And that is exactly how it turned out to be. The evening shift nurses gathered together to get report from the day shift. I sat in on report with the nurse that was orienting me. Just listening to some of the stuff that was said on report made me nervous. I had never been around someone dying, and had never even seen a dead body. I didn't even understand some of the stuff they were talking about. "What have I gotten myself into?" I thought. Before I could even answer that question in my head someone peeked into the report room and said, "Mr. Smith just died." Suddenly total panic set in because he was going to be one of our patients. We had to leave report and go "take care of him," whatever that meant. I knew I was not ready for this, but as I followed my mentor down the hallway I knew that I didn't have much choice. There was no time to slowly ease into it; I was going in headfirst. We walked into his room and I saw an elderly man just lying in bed with a pasty color to him, bluish lips, eyes closed, and obviously not breathing. It was very strange to see someone not breathing. He was alone, which I am glad for because I'm sure that my own face turned pretty white. It was eerie standing next to a dead body; almost surreal to me. My mentor brought me out of my trance and told me the procedure for after someone dies. The body is cleaned and made presentable for the family. If the patient has a roommate, which he did, the body is transported down the hall to a little private room where the family can gather. This was also out of respect for the roommate and his family. Through this entire procedure all I kept thinking was, "I can't believe this man is dead, I am actually touching and looking at a dead body." To be honest, it gave me the heebie-jeebies but I did not let my mentor see that. The image of that man's face stayed with me the rest of the day, so I don't remember much else about my first day. I went home really wondering if I could do this kind of work but knew that I had to give it more than one day. So, I got up the next morning and went back, hoping that no one would die that day. I actually didn't have to deal with any more deaths for a while, so I started to relax more. That gave me a chance to start learning about hospice care. I did not realize all the work that was involved in caring for hospice patients. There was a lot of education, knowledge, and skill required to keep them comfortable. I learned that it wasn't just about caring for the patient, but caring and supporting the family and friends who love them. I woke up every morning excited to go to work, wondering what I would learn and experience that day. I also looked forward to seeing the patients, their families, and the staff. It was like a family there. Seven years later I still wake up every morning and look forward to seeing and caring for my patients and their families. This is where my heart is.

I was amazed at how the whole staff worked together as a team. The nurses, aides, social workers, and chaplains do whatever it takes to make the patient and loved ones comfortable. The staff really supported each other; there were always hugs and laughter in the nurses' station. Occasionally I would see tears when a staff member would lose a patient they had connected with, but there was always plenty of support right there for them. It's a comfort knowing that when you are going through something like that there is no one who understands better than your co-workers because they have all been there a time or two. There didn't seem to be any egos, everyone loved their job and didn't think that one person was better than another (not that I noticed anyway). There was so much to learn but I did not find it overwhelming like at the hospital. I always thought you just gave them medicine and they died. I quickly realized that it is so much more than that. It was more than just medication; it was about treating the whole person, every single aspect of them, their life, and everyone who loves them. Everything was so laid back, nothing was ever rushed, there was no stress. I remember the founder of the hospice always saying, "There are no emergencies in hospice, so I never want to see anyone running or rushing around." Nurses were actually encouraged to sit with patients and talk, hold their hand, and give hugs when needed, and they actually had time to do these things. They took the time to sit down and educate the families about what was happening, what to expect, answer their questions, and listen to their concerns. The patients who were alone and had no one were the ones the staff would sit with and listen to their stories, and give them a gentle touch to let them know they weren't alone. Seeing this was truly amazing to me and it took me a while to feel comfortable doing it since it was frowned upon in the hospital, besides, you didn't have time anyway. As I walked around it hit me that every person in each one of these beds would die soon. That is when I decided I wanted to make sure that I did my best to make their last days the best they could be—to bring a smile to their face or make them laugh, to make the journey a little less scary for both the patient and their loved ones through education, caring, and listening. Then I realized that this kind of work is exactly why I went into nursing. I just never knew where to look for it.

# Hospice Nursing

"Why hospice nursing?" "Isn't it depressing?" "How can you do that?" These are the most frequently asked questions I hear when people find out that I am a hospice nurse. Some people aren't sure what to say, so they just look at me with wide eyes and opened mouths. Other people praise me and say that they admire the work that I do. Some share stories of their personal experience with hospice. Then there are the people who have no idea what hospice is, and after a little education they are too speechless to comment. The only time I have found that hospice (death and dying) can be talked about openly, lightheartedly, and even with some humor is between a group of hospice nurses. My fellow hospice nurses have been, and continue to be, such a huge support to me. We are always there for each other, whether it is for a hug, to dry someone's tears, giving reassurance that the right things are being done and encouragement during those difficult days, that we have all had, where you aren't sure if you can do this anymore. It isn't always an easy job, but it's nice to have colleagues who have been where you are and you know they truly understand. There will always be certain families and patients who tug at your heartstrings and some that really challenge and frustrate you. The important thing is that you never feel alone.

It has been said that there is a certain type of "hospice humor" that we all seem to acquire; something that just can't be explained. It can be pretty sick at times, but hospice nurses understand it. We understand that we need that time to unwind, laugh, and let go of the seriousness of the job we do. Believe it or not, there are some pretty hilarious things that happen around hospice but not everyone would see it the same way. I can remember many times while working in a hospice facility laughing so hard that my stomach ached and there were tears running down my face. It seemed like something funny was always happening to someone, and they would share it with everyone so we could all get a good laugh. We would also play jokes on each other and just do fun things to break up the intensity of what we do. At first, in the back of my mind I thought, "I can't believe I am laughing about this." After a while, though, that thought went away and I understood that the laughter was a type of release that we needed. The laughter was never done in an inappropriate place or at an inappropriate time, but I realized in hospice you have to be able to let go of the difficult situations and deaths because if you don't you will not survive. Let's face it, talking about death and dying isn't exactly joyful dinner conversation to most people. Hospice nursing is a passion. It is something you feel from your heart. You either have a calling for it or not, there is no in-between. I have seen many nurses start and leave after the first couple of deaths they have, "I just can't handle all the death," they would say. Some people focus so much on the death that they miss out on all the living that goes on in hospice. Hospice is about people who unfortunately have a terminal illness and an uncertain time to live—it could be days, weeks, months, or even years. Within that time, it is the hospice staff who make every day as physically comfortable as possible. They help emotionally heal people, and help them find peace within themselves and what they have done, or not done, with their lives, making them feel that they are still important and that their lives mean something despite the condition they are in now. Hospice has brought people together and fulfilled dreams. We have gotten the military to release someone to come back from overseas and spend the last few days with their dying loved one. We have also gotten people a pass out of jail to come visit a dying loved one, supervised by a police officer of course. Patients have taken trips to see loved ones or simply go back home to where they grew up. There have been some reunions of long lost family members and friends. Giving the patient a chance to make amends and say good-bye that would not have otherwise happened. Hospice has had volunteers go with some patients who had no one to their homes and help them go through stuff and get things finished that were unexpectedly left. Patients go on outings if they are able. The focus is on what we can do to make a certain dream come true, help fulfill unresolved issues, make them comfortable in every way, and just simply make them feel loved and important. If you focus on all that, hospice is not that depressing. It turns out to be quite rewarding after they die, because then you can look back and feel good about how you made their shortened life more complete and more comfortable than it would have been.

To work hospice you must be comfortable with your own mortality, and comfortable about your feelings of death and beliefs of what comes after. It doesn't matter if your beliefs come from a religion of any kind, a spiritual belief, or one that is unique to only you. Whatever it is, the important thing is that the belief must be able to give you strength and peace of mind to do this job. It is so rewarding because it gives you the privilege to reach out to people in their darkest and most frightening time in their lives to give them comfort and a hand to hold. You are there to care for the human spirit and help them on their journey. At the same time you are there to help prepare the loved ones who will be left behind. Hospice nursing is not about the latest technology, the newest surgical procedure, or new medications or treatments. It is about making the patients comfortable in their last weeks or days of life, doing whatever it takes to make that happen, and supporting and educating those who love them. It is not important whether you forget to take a blood pressure, temperature, or listen to every lobe of their lungs. What is important is that you keep your patient as comfortable as possible in all aspects, not just physically. If your patient is not comfortable, do everything you can to make them comfortable and keep them that way until the end. It is very important to educate and be honest with the people who are watching their loved one die. They deserve to know what is going on, what to do, and what to expect. Educate to the best of your knowledge, but realize that you aren't going to have all the answers because every situation is different even if several patients have the same illness. No one's journey through this is the same, just as in life. The loved ones need to fill supported and know that there is someone there twenty-four hours a day, seven days a week for them. They don't have to go through this alone and scared. All they need to do is reach out, and we will help carry them through this. Hospice nursing is about holding someone's hand when there are alone scared and have no one. Sometimes you have to listen to the same story a thousand times, and that's ok, because these people just want to be heard. They want to feel validated that they still matter—that who they are and what they did with their lives still matters.

The majority of hospice patients are stricken by cancer that has spread throughout their body. Some are lung diseases, such as emphysema. Others are starting to lose the long battle with MS, ALS, Parkinson's disease, or Alzheimer's. A few have made the difficult choice to stop dialysis after years of battling diabetes or kidney disease. There have been a couple of patients that were placed into hospice after they had been resuscitated after cardiac arrest and it left them in a vegetative state. The family wishes not to place them on life support. Once in a while there will be someone with end-stage AIDS but not as many as when I first started seven years ago, which is a good thing but still have a way to go in stopping it. There are a few with bad heart conditions and some that are elderly that have just given up, stopped eating and want to die. Some have had massive strokes that have left them in a vegetative state, along with some severe head injuries where the patient is declared brain dead; and the families have decided against life support. Unfortunately, there have been a few babies and children that come to hospice born with severe brain defects or other abnormalities that will not allow them to survive for long. Some people come to hospice because they have battled with alcoholism, and/or drug addiction leading to cirrhosis of the liver. Only once do I remember having a lady come to hospice with a type of the flesh-eating bacteria. She only survived a few days, which was a blessing for her because she was in so much pain and it was such an awful thing to see.

By the time someone reaches the point of needing hospice, most have gone through so much already—years filled with surgeries, treatments, chemotherapy, and the side effects that come with all those things. Everyone starts off with so much hope and then realizes that there is none. It is a very big adjustment for the patient and everyone who loves them. Some need patience and space to adjust and then when they are ready they get all the support they need. Others want all the support and education we can give them right away. Their life as they have always known it is gone. For loved ones of the patients, the person they once knew is gone, physically and sometimes mentally. The illness has consumed their once healthy, full of life body and mind, now just a shell of their former self, sometimes not even recognizable. Sometimes patients totally withdraw from everyone that they love. This is obviously very difficult for the loved ones to understand and emotionally accept. They need to know that sometimes dying patients withdraw in order to process everything that is happening to them. It is an overwhelming amount of stuff, and a very private thing that is happening to their bodies and minds and no one else's. Sometimes withdrawing is a sign that they are starting to prepare themselves and their loved ones for the day when it will be time to say good-bye. For some, being sick and dying is a very private thing, and they want to be alone. Others like to have everyone they love around them and need support and love from as many people as possible.

Some patients have come through a very long fight, often lasting years. They go through numerous surgeries and treatments that make them sick, and experimental drugs that no one really knows much about, yet they are willing to try everything. There is so much uncertainty, but they still have hope, not wanting to lose the battle, but knowing in their hearts they have already lost. They are reluctant to go into hospice because that means giving up, but as much as they want it not to be true; there is nothing else that can be done for them. Some people continue to fight up to the very last minutes of their lives, still not wanting to give up or let go. Denial is a powerful thing. These patients often have a lot of anxiety, and usually need to be medicated with anti-anxiety medications to be kept calm and comfortable. Others realize they have run out of options and that there is nothing more to do but to go into hospice and let go. Knowing that hospice will give them peace of mind because they will be taken care of and made comfortable, there is no longer any need to fight.

There are some patients who come to this point in their lives through some chronic condition that they have been living with for years, always knowing in the back of their minds what the eventual outcome will be. Sometimes they can be in denial too, thinking, "Since I have lived with this for so many years already and have been fine, I must have some more years left." Sometimes this is true, and these types of patients can turn into long-term patients whom we have had for up to three years. These types of patients are the only ones who actually have, on occasion, been discharged from hospice after showing no decline after a long period of time. Not many people can say that they have been discharged from hospice because they got better or their condition did not get any worse.

Then there are the patients who end up at hospice after their lives are changed in a blink of an eye. They are just like all of us, out there living, dreaming, working, and caring for their families. Then one day they complain of a headache that won't go away, so they go to the doctor, thinking nothing of it, get a CAT scan, and find that they have an aggressive brain tumor—the type of tumor that is so aggressive surgery will only make it spread faster and there is no treatment that will be able to slow it down or stop it. Suddenly the patient finds himself in the room with the doctor who tells them they only have days or weeks to live, and suggests hospice. The patient is admitted to hospice and dies a week later (that story is based on the death of an actual patient I took care of). There is also a story of a young man who was out skateboarding and got hit by a car. His family decided to remove the life support and move him to hospice. We have had patients who were just fine one minute, and the next had a massive stroke and ended up in hospice in an unresponsive state. I remember taking care of an elderly woman who had fallen and broken her hip. She was taken to the emergency room. They took x-rays and other tests, then determined that she had cancer all over her body and she didn't even know it. The family said this woman was never sick and never complained of feeling sick or anything until she fell. She had no visual signs of being sick at all. She was admitted to hospice and died two weeks later. It all happened so fast that the family was left with their heads still spinning, wondering, "What just happened? How could she go from a simple broken hip to dying of cancer?" Sometimes there just isn't any rational explanation for some of these circumstances.

With hospice nursing you don't just take care of the patient, you must care for the family and friends because they feel so helpless and scared as they watch their loved one die before their eyes. Some people realize that it is going to happen and want to be involved and educated, while others remain in denial up to the very end, not believing that this could be happening to their loved one. "Just last week she was driving and cooking three meals a day," they will say to me. Others express intense anger towards the doctor, hospital, or whatever circumstances may have contributed to the person's terminal illness. The best thing you can do is just listen to them and keep an open mind regarding their particular situation. Sometimes you have to grow a thick, but caring, skin, because a lot of the anger can easily be taken personally. Sometimes you get yelled at a lot just because you are there and are someone for them to vent to. Education is a large part of what we do, because it is usually in the hospital or clinic right after the prognosis is made that is the first time hospice is explained to the patient and loved ones. Obviously, they are still in shock about what they have just been told, so they don't retain a whole lot of what is said, if anything. So, it is a work in progress, reeducating on what hospice is and what the prognosis means, what the doctor told them, and sometimes what they weren't told. Every day is spent answering questions, sometimes the same questions over and over; having an open mind and listening to concerns and fears. Every day there is education to be done on what is happening to the patient, how to make them comfortable, and how to let their loved ones be as involved as they want to be and give them as much information and education as they want. Of course, it is important to respect those who don't want to be that involved, giving them just the information they wish to have, if any. If the family and/or patient wish to stay at home, there is a lot of education about how to care for a terminally ill patient at home. As their condition declines, educating the loved ones on how to care for their now bedbound loved one who can do nothing for themselves. Inevitable you will always be asked "the question." "When are they going to die?" With some people you really can tell, down to the hour sometimes; but others can be a surprise to you as much as to the family. Even though we don't have all the answers doesn't mean that we can't give good care and make the patient comfortable. And we don't need all the answers to still comfort in those times of fear. Hold the hand of the one who is scared and alone, hug those that are lost and need to feel safe, caring arms around them. Others need an open mind and kind ear for their thoughts to be heard. We must respect those that chose to run away or close themselves off from the situation. We need to meet the patient and loved ones where they are, individually as every situation is different. This is their journey after all, and they need to lead us, whether in sorrow, fear, regret, denial, anger, or acceptance. Just assure them that we will be walking right beside them until the end and all they need to do is reach out to us. Hospice nursing is like an adventure of the unexpected, especially when going out into people's homes. Whether there is major dysfunction or nothing but love, we must find a way to support the patient and family through this difficult time. Whether in a facility or at home; we must not forget to respect the family's beliefs and lifestyles, even if we do not agree with them. Hospice is not there to push beliefs or values on anyone; we are there to support everyone. Even though hospice nursing is very rewarding, it can also be very emotionally draining and sometimes heartwrenching. I'm sure there is not a hospice nurse out there who hasn't had those moments at the end of the day when you say to yourself, "I can't do this anymore!" But the rewards and praise outweigh these thoughts, and they pull you back in and you carry on. I once had a patient's wife come up to me, out of the blue, and give me a big hug and say, "That is for all you do, not just for me and my family but for all your patients and families, you are truly a special person." She must have known something, because that was the last time I saw her. Her husband died a few nights later. It made my heart melt, and validated that I am truly doing what I love. It's moments like those that make all the difficult ones fade away. I always want to take their pain away, especially when death nears and they start to realize that this is really happening. It is very difficult at times, but this is a natural part of the life cycle, and everyone is going to go through it sometime. Of course, when you are holding a sobbing spouse of a patient, that thought doesn't usually enter your mind. Therefore, my goal is to make death as comfortable and peaceful as possible for the patient, and the least frightening for the loved ones as possible. Some days there is a place in my heart that aches and realizes that any one of these situations could easily be happening to me or someone I love, and that no one is immune and life is precious. I walk into these people's homes, entering their lives at the most painful time, and I feel privileged that they are allowing me to do so. It's amazing, because I don't look at my patients and think, "Oh, this person is going to die of cancer." Instead, I think about how I can make this patient's and family's day better. I take things day by day, and hope that in some small way I can make that day a little brighter or a little less painful and scary. Sometimes I walk out of the house after the patient and/or family has brightened my day with their courage, sense of humor, and amazing spirit.

The most difficult moment for me is always when it comes time to take my stethoscope, place it over the heart, and listen for one minute to confirm the death. Most of the time it is very obvious that they are gone, but it is procedure. The loved ones are always right there, staring at you with eager eyes, hoping that somehow there will be a heartbeat, and somehow they are not really gone. Sometimes the families and loved ones still seem to have that little bit of hope left, even if they haven't seen them breathe for minutes and sometimes even hours. They hold onto that hope until they see you check with your stethoscope, then look up into their eyes and tell them that their loved one is gone. At that moment is when a lot of people finally realize that their loved one has died. It is a surreal experience that causes an eerie feeling when you have your stethoscope over someone's heart; a heart that for years beat with a rhythm giving someone life, but is now silent, forever. The chest that once moved up and down giving the breath of life now remains still, never to breathe again.

# *Journey of the Unknown*

Your journey is filled with fear and uncertainty
Your mind is constantly searching for some kind of reason
For why this is so,
And you wonder how you will ever find the strength
And courage to make it through another day

Your illness has become you
And you no longer recognize yourself or the life you once had
Never taking the time to realize that you are still the person you have always been
All you have to do is look into your heart
And you will find the true you is still there
And no illness can take that from you

You feel as if everything has been taken from you
And you are filled with anger
For everything you have worked for is now lost
But not realizing that the most important things can never be taken from you
Because they are in your heart
And you take them with you

As the sun sets on yet another day
Your fear starts to grow
Bedtime is no longer filled with good dreams
Now each night
Before you close your eyes
You wonder if it will be your last

You feel so completely alone in the dark of the night
And as the tears fall from your cheeks
You feel a gentle hand
The hand wraps around yours

Your hand that was once strong
But is now so frail

As you open your eyes
You realize that your hospice nurse is holding your hand
Sitting right beside you on the edge of your bed
No words are exchanged,
The touch says it all
And as you slowing drift off to sleep
You realize you are not alone

It is painful for you to watch your loved ones stare down at you
As you lie helplessly and frail in bed
Each one of them with tears in their eyes
You never wanted them to ever feel this kind of pain
And you wonder if they realize that your heart aches too
Because you know that you will be leaving them soon

For each beginning there is an ending
And this is the end of one journey
And the beginning of another
A journey that is unknown
And can be frightening
But hospice is there to make sure that you and your loved ones don't go
Through this journey alone
We are there to make it as comfortable and peaceful as possible
And to make sure no one ever feels alone and scared

# Words of Inspiration

Carol was the first patient who really made an impact on me. It was about six years ago. I had only been working with hospice patients for about a month or two. I was still learning every day and had not had to deal with many deaths yet, and I hadn't really connected with any of the families or patients until Carol. I was working in a hospice facility at the time and before I ever took care of her I would hear the other nurses say what a difficult, mean patient she was to take care of. This, of course, scared me, being new and not having cared for many patients, let alone a difficult one. Well, it came to be my turn to take care of her, and I prepared myself for the worst. I must say she was a very stubborn elderly lady who had throat cancer, which required her to have a trach (a plastic device placed in her throat with a hole in it that allowed her to breathe). Carol was a tiny little woman, weighing probably about eighty pounds at the most, and was not much over five feet tall. She was not very patient and was difficult to understand, which frustrated both her and everyone trying to care for her. I remember if people said "what?" to her enough, she somehow got the strength to very clearly and loudly make her needs known. She wanted things her way and wanted them now. She could be very demanding at times. Most of the staff did not get along very well with her. The more time I spent with her and the more patient I was with her, the easier I found her to get along with. Of course, when the rest of the staff learned of this I ended up caring for her a lot. I eventually looked forward to caring for her even though she could still be challenging at times. Those days when she was being particularly challenging and impatient I would try to put myself in her position. I probably wouldn't be the most pleasant person either. As time went on, it became easier to understand her and we communicated just fine. I even got her to smile a few times. There were days when I wasn't her nurse, but whoever was caring for her would always come and get me if they were having a hard time understanding her. When I would walk into her room with her nurse with me, she would always look up at me and smile, as if to say, "Finally, someone who can understand me."

She was there for quite a while, and I began to bond with her only daughter who would come every evening to be with her mom. Her daughter would even say that her mother could be a difficult person and praised my patience with her. Carol was short of breath all the time, and every breath she took was a struggle. The most comfortable position for her was when she had her head hanging forward towards her chest. I would ask her if her neck hurt, and she always said no. I don't understand how she could breathe through her trach like that, but she did somehow. She would sometimes bend at the hips and lean forward. It looked like she was folded in half. She could stay in this position for long periods of time. She would usually sleep like that. If you tried to straighten her, she would very clearly let you know that she did not like that. We were all amazed at how flexible this little lady was. Every time you would walk past her room and see her like that you would want to go in there and straighten her up, but you knew that for some reason she was comfortable like that. Her condition remained stable for a few months or so longer than anyone ever thought she would last. She never really ate much but was constantly drinking coffee and she would even find a way to drink her coffee with her head bent forward. The only time she would allow her head to be in the upright position was when her trach would have to be cleaned because she knew it had to be done. Carol did not show any of the physical symptoms of a declining condition. She always seemed to be pretty much the same, so I was shocked when I returned to work after two days off and was barely in the door when I saw Carol's daughter running towards me. She threw her arms around me and just started sobbing, "Mom's dying!" Of course, my mind and heart were going ninety miles an hour, because this was the first experience I had had like this and wasn't sure how to handle it or if I could handle it. There was a part of me that thought, "I can't do this type of work if it is always going to be like this." Then I snapped myself back into reality and knew that I had a job to do right now and would have to think later. So I took a deep breath, pulled myself together, and went on. It was either that or completely fall apart, run from the building, and never look back. I knew I couldn't do that because I had to be there for Carol and her daughter. She obviously looked to me to help her through this. After hugging for what seemed like forever, her daughter said, "I am so glad you are here, you are so good with Mom, I think she was waiting for you." This brought a tear to my eye, but again I knew I had to keep it together. My tears would have to wait. I walked into her room with her daughter and was amazed because Carol was actually lying down on her back in the bed, straightened out with her head elevated a little bit. Her eyes were closed, and she looked so peaceful. She finally looked comfortable to me, even though she said she was always comfortable bent forward. Her breathing was slow and both the daughter and I knew it wouldn't be long. I continued to medicate her as needed to keep her comfortable, and about one hour before my shift ended she passed away with her daughter at her bedside. Her daughter came to get me then, and I had the awful duty of listening for a heartbeat for one full minute, then looking into her eyes and telling her that her mother was gone. This was very difficult, because her daughter was on the other side of the bed directly across from me, still holding her mother's hand. I could feel her eyes watching me, and I wasn't ready to look up yet. The minute passed and I heard nothing. I removed the stethoscope from Carol's chest, looked at her daughter, and said, "I'm sorry, she's gone." The daughter just sat there holding her mother's hand crying softly. I left the room to give them some time alone and also to give myself some time away from the first tear-jerking situation of my hospice career. Walking down the hallway to the nurses' station, I kept thinking, "Boy, this is really hard, I don't know if I can do this." The other nurses reassured me that not every death would be like this. They told me that even though you get used to it, there would always be some patients who touch your heart more than others do, and those are always difficult.

With that advice in mind, I went back down to Carol's room. Her body was gone by then, and her daughter was gathering up her things. She gave me one last big hug and said quietly in my ear, "You were so good with Mom, I couldn't have gotten through this without you, thank you so much. I can see you have a gift for this kind of work and are very good at it. Don't ever forget that. This is where you belong so stay with it, and don't get discouraged." I will never forget those words, and that is the moment when I realized I was meant to be a hospice nurse. I am so glad I decided not to go running from the building that day.

This experience taught me that everyone's perception of a "difficult patient" is different. Regardless of whatever the perception is, the patient still deserves the same type of care as everyone else. When you are feeling frustrated and wanting to pull all your hair out and never go back in the patient's room again whether it is because of the patient or the family, take a deep breath and remember that they are only human and that their life has ended as they have known it. They might be scared but just don't know how to express it. Be patient with them and imagine for a second what it would be like if that was you or someone you loved. No one can possibly truly understand what these patients go through physically or emotionally. That is all the more reason to treat everyone with respect and dignity and not to take their anger personally.

# The Light

Larry was a patient I took care of about five years ago. He lived with his wife of only six years. It was the second marriage for him but it was her first. She had finally met the love of her life. She told me how she had given up on ever finding someone to be with and love, and then she met him. They were both in their late fifties and he had two grown children from his first marriage. She had never had children. He was diagnosed with colon cancer about one year before and had undergone more than one surgery and chemotherapy. The chemotherapy was unsuccessful, and the cancer continued to grow and spread at such a rapid rate that the doctor told him there was nothing else that could be done. His prognosis was less than six months, and he reluctantly agreed to be admitted into hospice. He came into hospice still adjusting to the fact that everything he had gone through was unsuccessful. All of his hope and courage to fight the cancer were gone. The cancer had won and taken over his body. His wife was still in the shock and denial phase and was not ready for hospice. She, like many people, still had the hope that there must be something else out there the doctors could do to save him. But, unfortunately, as much as she wanted that to be true, it wasn't. There was nothing else they could do.

The first time I met him and his wife they were still bitter about the prognosis and were not exactly happy to see me. Of course, not many families greet me with open arms. They were very closed off and unfriendly towards me. I could hear the anger in their voices when they spoke to me, and all I could do at the beginning was listen and empathize. They talked about how he struggled through surgeries and the sickness of the chemotherapy. He faced all of it for the last year with such courage, willing to do whatever it took to beat the cancer. They were angry about how the doctor kept giving them so much hope, when in reality there was none. They had questions about whether he had received the right surgery and the right chemotherapy treatments. They had so many "what if?" questions. While listening to everything they had been through, I watched how they looked at each other. I realized how much they loved each other and that there was no way I could ever understand what they were going through. I knew that I could still listen and support them. I offered them the support of a chaplain, social worker, nurse's aide, or volunteer. They refused all of it and they only wanted me out there. So, I was on my own, wearing all the hats without the usual support of my other hospice team members, but I had to respect their wishes.

Over time he slowly started accepting the progression of his illness and his prognosis. He expressed to me that he was so glad to be able to stay at home and was, in a way, relieved that there would be no more invasive procedures or medicines that would make him sick. He started opening up to me and we built a good relationship that was filled with laughter and good conversation. His wife was still not ready to accept that the love of her life was going to die. She would always leave the room during my visits. She would only greet me at the door and show me out, saying nothing. She did not want to hear anything I said and I respected that. He would tell me that she was not ready to face the reality of what was happening. He said he would even try and talk with her but she would hear nothing of it. He was very concerned about her and loved her very much. I tried to reassure him that she would eventually come around. I tried to get him to see things through her eyes. He was her life, the love she had waited so long to find. Now after only a short time together she was going to lose him. She was watching the man she loved die before her eyes. She was feeling very helpless and angry, because she knew there was nothing she could do to stop it. My heart ached for both of them. He knew he was going to die. He said he was not afraid of dying but didn't want to leave her because he loved her and didn't know if she would be ok. She remained distant for quite some time, but she slowly started warming up to me and started sitting at the table with us. She still didn't say much but she was making small steps and I continued to be patient with her and give her the space she needed.

The three of us would eventually have really nice conversations and he would always make us laugh. He would have at least one joke for me every time I came for a visit, which was twice a week. He seemed to be facing the most frightening thing in his life with such courage and peace. I still remember sitting at that cherrywood dining room table visiting with them and laughing before I did my nursing assessment. I would ask him how he was feeling, to which he would always reply, "How do I feel? With my hands." He was a funny man, always with smartmouth answers to my questions. He loved to tease me and give me a hard time about everything and anything. I didn't feel offended and I didn't mind because it made us both laugh. He always had a big clear glass bowl of cherries in front of him that he would sit and eat. Cherries still remind me of him. It's strange the things that stick with you about someone.

I had only been caring for him for a few months when his condition started to decline. His pain was always kept under control with morphine, and he never had any nausea or vomiting. It seemed like overnight he became very weak and started losing a lot of weight. I knew something was wrong when he could no longer meet me at the dining room table and eat cherries. After he became so weak he could no longer walk or get out of bed, he seemed to just give up—he was ready to go. I had to put a Foley catheter into his bladder because his body no longer knew how to urinate, so the urine would stay in his bladder, which caused him pain. The tube constantly drains the urine to keep the bladder empty. He no longer wanted to eat or drink and would sleep most of the time, all of which is normal for the dying process, but he would wake up long enough to tell me a joke when I came for my visits. This was when his wife started to realize that this was really going to happen. She would always be sitting on the bed next to him while I checked him over and asked how he was doing. She always kept him very comfortable, and his only complaint was how he hated just lying in bed not able to do anything. "This is not living," he would say. After I finished my visit with him, his wife and I would go into the kitchen and talk. She would ask questions about what was going on and what was going to happen. Of course she would always ask the most frequent question I am asked, "When is he going to die?" I was as honest as I could be with her because I knew that she needed that, but I simply did not have the answer to that question. After talking, she would squeeze my hand or pat me on the shoulder and thank me for everything I had done for both of them. She wasn't the kind of person who warmed up to others easily, so I knew she wasn't ready for a hug and I would let her reach out to me first. She would always say, "You are such a big support to me, I don't know what I would do without you." Then her eyes would fill with tears and she would say, "He is my best friend, the love of my life, what am I going to do without him?" She never cried in front of him, "I have to be strong for him," she would say. All I could do was hold her hand, let her cry, and try to comfort her in some way. This was difficult because I couldn't possibly know what she was going through. Seeing the sorrow in her eyes was difficult for me, and there were many times that I fought back my own tears.

With each visit I saw that his condition was declining more and I had to tell her that the time was getting closer. I think in her heart she knew but just didn't want to face it. I had always seen him on the same days at the same times. One day his wife called about one hour before I was to visit him. I didn't think anything of it and thought she probably had a question or needed something before I got out there. I remember that on my previous visit I knew his condition was continuing to decline but nothing told me death was imminent. I would have given him a couple more weeks, that's why the phone call did not alarm me. When I called her back she was sobbing so hard I could barely understand her. I got her to calm down so I could understand what was going on. She said, "He told me he was dying and he told me to call you because he said he is waiting for you but doesn't think he can wait much longer. Please hurry!" On my way over to the house I thought that he was probably just getting confused or having some anxiety. She greeted me at the door with a tear-stained face and again said, "He keeps saying he is waiting for you." Even at this point I thought that he was having some confusion or anxiety. It didn't hit me until I walked into the bedroom and saw that he was very close to death. This amazed me because his wife said that from the time she called me until I drove up to the house he was very much alert and oriented. There was no confusion. He knew exactly what he was saying and what was happening to him. When she came back from letting me in was when he became nonresponsive. His breathing was very labored, and he had long periods between breaths when he would not breathe (apnea) and his color was gray. He was lying in the middle of their king-size bed with his eyes closed. He looked very peaceful. There were no signs of pain, anxiety, or discomfort of any kind. Standing there looking at him made me feel so good because I knew he was comfortable due to the things I did to control his symptoms. My heart was aching at the same time because I knew I would never hear a joke from him again. He had touched my heart, and I was going to miss him. I climbed onto the bed and took his cold, blue hand in mine, gave it a gentle squeeze, and told him that I was there now. I felt a very slight squeeze back, but he never opened his eyes. His wife had climbed on the bed too and was holding his other hand. As gently and subtly as I could, I told her that he was very close to death. She said nothing, she just put her head next to his and started crying, "Please don't leave me, I'm not ready yet, I love you so much." I felt so helpless because I knew this man was going to die soon. There was nothing I could do to save the man she loved or take her pain away. I had to constantly choke down my own tears because I was witnessing such love between two people who had just found each other and now were about to be separated by death. I kept watching his breathing and concentrating on the time as the time between breaths became longer. I had to tune out what she was saying to him because it was so heartwrenching and I had to stay professional. This was difficult because I had a big lump in my throat to constantly remind me of my own emotions.

His breathing was slowing, when suddenly out of the corner of my eye I saw a subtle flash of white light appear in the far corner of the room, then it just disappeared. I thought maybe it was a light from outside but it wasn't near a window and the curtains were closed. I didn't think anything of it until later that day. I will leave you to draw your own conclusions. At the same time I saw the light, I happened to look down at him and noticed he was no longer breathing. My heart just dropped. His wife's head was buried, face down, in the nook between his head and shoulder, and I knew she had not noticed he was gone. I could hear her mumbling, over and over, "I'm not ready yet, don't go." I slowly got off the bed and went to get my stethoscope to check for a heartbeat. His wife lifted her head for the first time in a long while. She just looked at me with sad, lost eyes, as if to say, "Please don't let him go." I thought to myself, "Believe me, if I had the power I wouldn't let him go and I would take away all your pain, but I don't have that power." I listened for one minute, which is usually what I do, but I listened to him for at least two minutes because I was trying to gather my strength to look into her eyes and tell her he was gone. I finally had to do it. I removed the stethoscope from his chest and looked into her eyes and said softly, "I'm sorry, he's gone." She fell on top of him and cried, mumbling, "No, no, no!" "I'm not ready yet!" over and over. At that point, I could no longer hold in my tears. I sat there beside him and quietly wept for a while and then quickly wiped away my tears and composed myself. I wept for all her pain, but I also wept for me because I lost a patient I had grown to enjoy and care about. I knew I had to get out before my emotions took over me. I had phone calls to make and had to sound professional, plus I wanted to give her some time alone with him.

After calling the mortuary I knew I had about an hour before they would get there. "How am I going to handle this for an hour?" I thought to myself. I just took a deep breath and went back into the bedroom. The wife was no longer crying; she was just sitting next to his head on the bed. I came in and said someone from the mortuary would be there in about an hour. She nodded. Her eyes looked so empty to me, I did not see the sadness or fear like I did before. There was no life in them anymore. I then sat in a chair by the bed and did my charting. After a few seconds of awkward silence, the wife started talking to me. She told me how they met, what kind of person he was, and all about their short life together. I heard about the adventures they had and the dreams they had that would now go unfulfilled. The more she talked to me about him the more it seemed to calm her, which calmed me too. She held it together pretty well when they took his body, and even after they were gone. I watched her the whole time and there was no expression to her face or eyes; she looked like a doll. It was as if the life in her went with him when he died.

I then started to gather up my things and let her know I was going. She put her arms around me and gave me a big, long hug and thanked me for everything. When she hugged me I knew in my heart that I had helped her through this, in some way, even if just a little bit. She thanked me for the support and laughter I had given both of them during the last months of his life. She told me that he did not warm up to many people but he talked about how much he liked me and enjoyed my visits and looked forward to seeing me. He told her how good it felt to sit and laugh with me and give me a hard time about everything, because for those short seconds I would make him forget about what was happening. She told me that she also enjoyed my visits and thanked me for all the support and about being honest with her. It was difficult to leave her because she was all alone now, without the man that she loved. She assured me she would be ok and would call a friend to come stay with her. I knew that my work there was done and I had to get in my car and move on to the next patient and family that needed me. So, I slowly turned and walked out the door after one last hug. When I turned around she had closed the door but I could see that she was watching me out the kitchen window. I stared back at her and thought, "I never would have guessed they would have touched me so much." He continues to be the only patient for whom I was actually there when he died, and I find it quite an honor that he wanted me there and waited for me. Knowing I made him comfortable, helped him on his journey, and was able to help his wife through this horrible time in her life is what makes my job so rewarding.

This experience was the first of many that showed me that if the first meeting doesn't go well not to turn and run. Be patient and don't let first impressions get the best of you because they are usually wrong. Give them time to get to know you and open up. After all, you are coming into their homes and their private lives at the most awful time they could ever imagine. They have every right not to greet you with open arms at first.

Larry himself taught me about the strength of the spirit, the will to hang on, and dying the way you want to. Larry wanted me there that day, I truly believe that, and he had waited for me. He could have easily died right before I got there or later when I left. Loved ones should never feel guilty for going to the bathroom or taking a short break only to find that the patient has passed away while they were gone. If they want you there, they will make sure you are there with them.

# *Angels*

Gail was a patient I took care of about four years ago, and she turned out to be one who will always hold a special place in my heart. She was a spunky Irish lady with red hair, lots of freckles, a pale complexion, and green eyes that had a sparkle in them I will never forget. We hit it off right away because I am Irish with red hair too. She was in her seventies with a grown son. Her husband had passed away a few years before. She was so full of life. She was so funny and loved to laugh and talk. Gail was very easygoing and didn't take anything too seriously, including her prognosis. Her best friend lived next door and was always there for my visits helping to take care of her. They had been best friends for a long time, raised their children together and had both lost their husbands to cancer. They were each other's strength. Gail had been diagnosed with colon cancer about a year and a half before I met her. She had surgery, which left her with a colostomy bag (an external bag attached to part of the intestine that has been brought through the skin to expel waste into the bag). She chose not to have any further treatment. She was very at peace with her prognosis and with hospice. I took care of her for almost a year, which is a long time with that diagnosis.

The first day I met her I could tell she was far from giving up. I saw her twice a week and remember the experience like it was yesterday. I am still able to see her face, especially her smile and her sparkling green eyes. She would always be sitting in her recliner in front of a bay window, her best friend on the couch, and I would sit in another chair opposite her. Her son lived downstairs, and he would be walking around the house and would sometimes come and sit with us. Her best friend's daughter was also there most of the time. She was the same age as Gail's son; they grew up together and were like brother and sister. I felt very comfortable there and I enjoyed sitting and talking with them before having to take her blood pressure and pulse and listen to her lungs, heart, and stomach. I would also ask her how she was feeling, eating, and how her pain was. I would then check her colostomy and the skin under it and around it. Gail had had the colostomy for almost two years, so it was like part of her body now. She never made a fuss or a big deal about it. Her son and friend had been changing it since she got it so they were experts. Gail could not change it because it was in such an awkward place for her to reach it and see it. They actually knew more than I did, so I would watch them and they taught me a few tricks about how to keep it securely on and keep the skin in good condition. This procedure usually turned into quite the entertainment. Something funny would always happen or someone would say something funny and we would all be laughing before long. Sometimes it would be because they put it on wrong or forgot to do something. Meanwhile, Gail would be lying there laughing, saying "I can't believe I let you guys touch me!" She would tell me about all the times they didn't put it on right and "accidents would happen," and, of course, most of the time they were out in public. Gail would also tell me that her son would like to make up new concoctions and experiments to try and make it work better. Very few of his experiments worked, however. She always made me laugh. Imagine for a moment that someone who is dying is making you laugh—amazing. She did have pain, which I kept well controlled with morphine. The nausea and vomiting was pretty severe, though, and she took that in stride like everything else. This was a challenge for me, because I had never had a patient with nausea and vomiting so severe and difficult to control. All the usual medications that were used for this in hospice didn't help her at all. I felt so badly because it took me so long to find some relief for her. She tried so many different medications and was willing to keep trying, and with each one that failed she continued to keep her spirits up and kept her faith in me that I would find something that worked. I finally ended up using three different medications together on a regular basis to control it. I had finally done it, the medications together were working and she went weeks without any nausea or vomiting, and she could keep her food and fluids down. She went for almost a month or more, but then once in a while she would have a day when she would vomit almost continuously until she received a powerful shot of anti-nausea medication (Inapsine) which was effective and worked quickly. I would always breathe a big sigh of relief when she would tell me she was having no nausea or vomiting and felt fine. It was such a good feeling to know that it was my hard work, perseverance, and knowledge that was able to make her comfortable. She always had such faith in me and would tell me, "I'm not scared because I know that you will make me comfortable and be with me 'til the end." She always had a great big smile to greet me and in my mind I always thought, "How miserable she must be, how can she still be smiling and laughing?" She never really complained about anything that was happening to her.

As the months went by, I could see the cancer taking its toll on her body. She started losing a lot of weight, her appetite was declining some, but she was still eating her favorite foods. She became very weak and forgetful. Later on she starting becoming confused and she knew it. She loved to joke around about "losing her mind" and being confused. She would also joke around about how she was unsteady on her feet and would walk like she was drunk. She was constantly laughing at herself. When she knew she was confused she would purposely make up things and made everyone laugh, including herself. Even though she was confused, she always knew when I was coming to see her and she knew the day and month because she started setting goals for herself. The first couple of goals I thought were realistic but after that I thought, "There is no way she can make that one." Her first goal was Halloween because she loved children. She had her house decorated and insisted that she hand out the candy herself. That really made her tired so she slept most of the following day. She was slow to recover from activities now but always said it was worth it. Next goal was Christmas, I remember her face would light up just talking about Christmas. She really had her house decorated for Christmas. She went all out and continued to be upbeat even though she and everyone else knew it would be her last Christmas. I thought after Christmas was over she would pass away. But no, she had more goals in mind even though her condition was declining by the week. I was able to continue to keep her symptoms under control and she was very comfortable. She wanted to be around to ring in the New Year and she told me she had a little party with friends and her son and they stayed up and watched Dick Clark. That excitement took her almost a week to recover; she was getting so frail and weak. I was shocked to hear that her New Year's resolution was to live to St. Patrick's Day, being Irish and all. I remember feeling disappointed for her because I could see that physically I knew she could not make it. Of course, I didn't have the heart to tell her that so all I could do was encourage her.

St. Patrick's Day was a little more than two months away. Now with every visit I could see more decline. Gail had so much determination that I don't think she actually realized how sick she was. She still acted like the day I met her except for her confusion that she thought was pretty funny. She was so weak and could barely walk anymore and when she did she needed help and could only walk very short distances. Her nausea and vomiting were more under control now, but she was also taking in very little food or fluids. All of the symptoms she was experiencing are expected and the normal progression of terminal patients. She spent a lot of time sleeping and now had a hospital bed set up in the dining room area just off the living room. She wanted to be in her recliner for my visits. Her son said that she could only sit up for a few hours a day, then she would get too tired and have to go to bed. Some days she was more confused than others, but continued to know me and when I was coming. She still had that sparkle and spunk in her eyes. I was truly amazed when it was St. Patrick's Day and she was still hanging on and had the house decorated and was wearing green. She looked so happy—she had made it! After that her condition rapidly declined. She became bedbound and too weak to walk, and slept most of the time. She would still smile at me and I knew she still recognized me, but she didn't have enough strength to talk. She was so thin that sometimes I would look at her and she wouldn't even look like the same person, except for that sparkle in her eyes.

In the early morning of March twenty-third, just six days after St. Patrick's Day, I was paged and knew in my heart that she was gone. Her son confirmed it when I called. She lived about thirty to forty minutes away from me, and I wanted the drive to last forever because I was already holding back tears and wasn't sure if I could walk into that house, be professional, and do my job. I had the biggest lump in my throat the whole time. Even though I was alone in my car I knew I could not cry yet because I would not be able to stop. I pulled up to the house, and as I was walking up to the door I could already feel the energy—the house was different. I had to pause, take a deep breath and tell myself "You can do this, you have to be strong." When I walked in I automatically turned to her recliner, and it was empty. It was so strange not seeing her sitting there and even stranger that she never would be again. She was straight ahead of me lying in the hospital bed. Seeing her from a distance made me swallow hard and I had to tell myself "You can do this, stay strong." I knew I had to go listen for a heartbeat to confirm that she had passed away. All of the sudden it was like a dream—everything was cloudy white and misty. All I could see clearly was the path I had to walk from the door to her bed. It was just her and me. There were times as I started to walk towards her that I actually thought it was a dream. I don't even remember the family or friends being there. When I saw her it actually took my breath away because it didn't even look like her. It was very eerie to see someone who had been so full of life suddenly be so still. I did not expect my reaction to be that strong, and that suddenly made it more difficult to hold my tears back. The son and her best friend and her daughter had cleaned her, fixed her up, and placed a beautiful white lace handkerchief over her face. I did not have the courage to look underneath it, seeing through it was enough. There was a part of me that wanted to believe that it wasn't her because it didn't look like her, but I knew it was. I have never seen someone look so different. As I placed my stethoscope on her chest, I could not bring myself to look at her face so I just looked straight down at her still chest, where her wonderful, caring heart once beat. When I made my phone calls I noticed that my voice was cracking and I was close to just breaking down into sobs, but I continued to hold it back. When the mortuary representative came to take her body, her son and friends were grieving appropriately. As I was saying my good-byes, the son told me that Gail had left something for me and he handed me an angel pin, a butterfly necklace with a diamond-like stone in the middle, and a shamrock necklace. He gave me a hug, thanked me a thousand times for the wonderful care I had given his mother, and invited me to the funeral. As I walked to my car the whole experience seemed surreal. Driving home, I was surprised that I didn't cry. I think I was just too emotionally drained. I went home and slept a few hours before having to get up and go to work. When I walked into the office I was met by the most wonderful supervisor I have had the privilege of working with. She knew Gail had died and knew the connection I had with her. I remember standing just inside the door and saying in a quiet little voice, "She's gone." My supervisor just put her arms around me and at that was the moment when I went weak and started to cry. Everything I fought so hard to keep inside came out. I no longer had the strength to be strong, and knew that I no longer had to be. My supervisor sent me home that day, realizing I needed some sleep and some time to process everything. She was very right.

I went to Gail's funeral, which was beautiful, and I felt honored because I was mentioned in the service. Afterwords her son gave me a red rose from her casket, thanked me for coming, gave me a big hug, and told me how much I meant to her and everyone who loved her. Then her best friend came up to me gave me a hug and said, "Gail talked about you a lot. She really cared about you and liked you. You meant so much to her and she would look forward to seeing you. She used to say that you were her special angel sent directly to her to care for her until the end." As a tear ran down my cheek I looked in her best friend's eyes and said, "Now she can be my angel." At that moment I felt a sense of peace in my heart, something I hadn't felt since she died. The angel pin she left for me is hanging over my head in my car, a reminder that she is now my special angel watching over me.

Gail showed me the power of setting goals for yourself and having the will to achieve them. Whether it is to live until Christmas or win Olympic gold medal, you can do it if you put your mind to it. She also made me realize that you can make a big impact on someone's life by just being yourself and not even realizing it. I never knew how much she counted on me, trusted me, and cared for me until after she was gone. It wasn't until I talked with her best friend at her funeral that I found out just how much I meant to her. I silently thanked her for that, and I hope that some way she knows just what a big impact she had on me and my life.

# Too Young to Die

Most hospice patients are older or elderly—people who have been given a chance to live their lives. They have gotten married, raised children, had long careers, retired, and some have even had a chance to see the world. Many have had the chance to enjoy grandchildren and sometimes great-grandchildren. But once in awhile we get a young patient with their whole life ahead of them, dealing with a terminal illness too soon, having to face death when they should be facing life and looking forward to a future. These patients are the ones who really make you realize how fragile life is, and how life can make an unexpected and unexplained turn down a road no one would have ever imagined. One day you are a healthy young person doing what young people do and in a blink of an eye you find yourself sick and facing death, wondering "What just happened to my life?" "Why me?" I have learned that no human being is immune from getting a terminal illness, regardless of age. Even those with the healthiest of lifestyles, spending their whole life eating healthfully, exercising, doing "everything right," may still find themselves facing a terminal illness. It leaves you shaking your head, wondering "Why some and not others?" Or "Why now, why so young?" These are questions that have no answers. Stories like this one make me realize how easily it could be any one of us or someone we know.

Caring for young patients is difficult on everyone. Sometimes at meetings no one really knows what to say so there is a lot of silence and shaking of heads in disbelief. It is especially difficult when you are called upon to take care of someone who is either your age or very close to it. Bob was the first young patient I took care of. After a meeting, my supervisor pulled me aside before I made my first visit to the patient and she said, "This might be a difficult one for you, but I know you can do it, and don't forget that I am here for you if you need support. If it ever becomes too much let me know and I will put another nurse out there." After a speech like that I was petrified to care for this patient. I was still fairly new to home hospice; I had only been doing it for about two years or less. Bob was one or two years younger than I was. This made me feel a little awkward, because up to that time all my patients had been elderly people with a lifetime behind them. I wondered how Bob and his loved ones were going to respond to someone around the same age as him coming to take care of him. Would they have any confidence in my ability to do my job effectively? Were they going to believe I knew what I was talking about? Would they think, "How is a young nurse going to help support us through this?" "What does she know?" It was very intimidating. I knew that I had to go into this situation with lots of confidence and act like I had been doing this for one hundred years and not two. I did have my doubts about that strategy working, but it did. Before I knew it, Bob's family and friends were looking to me for answers. I could answer most of their questions but there were some questions I just didn't have the answers for. I could tell that when I talked to them they would really listen to me and take what I told them seriously. They were very understanding when I would occasionally have to say, "I just don't know." Although it was a lot of pressure because they relied on me to provide very important information about Bob's condition, it also made me feel good that they were comfortable and confident in me to care for someone who meant a lot to them.

Even before I made my first visit to him, this patient made me think about things my other patients hadn't. One day I was thinking of how strange life is. "Here I am driving around this beautiful city from house to house caring for the terminally ill, having a job I love, my health and having a future to look forward to. All my friends are out there too living their lives and doing the things that people in their twenties do," I was saying to myself. Then I realized that at the very same moment I knew of a twenty-six-year-old man who was dying of AIDS, his high school sweetheart taking care of him twenty-four hours a day. Something just didn't seem right; and to think that not long ago he was like everyone else in their twenties. He was working a full-time job, going out with friends, living with the woman he loves and just living life, never knowing what was lurking around the corner, and never imagining that around that soon he would be diagnosed with a terminal illness and forced to face his mortality. What was even more disturbing was that no one knew how he contracted the disease. I can't even begin to try to understand the question, "Why him?" I realize that it could just as easily be one of my friends, and I wondered how I would deal with that. Would I ever have the strength and courage that Bob's girlfriend and friends did? Remembering their love, support, and devotion for their friend still amazes me and brings tears to my eyes. What wonderful, loving people they all were, as they stood by helplessly and watched their friend die at such a young age. Having it all happen so fast and never knowing how or why, I wonder if his loved ones have ever had that question answered.

The day Bob was admitted to hospice, the doctors were still in the process of investigating all the possibilities, and trying to figure out how this healthy young man got AIDS and why it had progressed so rapidly. Before going to do my first visit, I read through his history and found that there was no evidence he had ever participated in any high-risk behaviors, never had a blood transfusion, and had done nothing that would link him to getting this deadly virus. Of course, there was a tiny, curious part of me that thought that maybe he had a secret in his past that he planned on taking to his grave. If he did, he succeeded in doing just that. After thinking about that, I actually felt guilty for having that thought about him. After all, it doesn't matter how he contracted it. The important thing is to help him through this, keep him comfortable, and support his family, friends, and loved ones through this terribly difficult time. Bob was a human being after all, a young one who was dying, and his loved ones were having to stand by and watch it all happen. It occurred to me that it doesn't matter how anyone "gets" their terminal illness, AIDS, cancer, or anything else. What matters is meeting the patient and family where they are at this moment, not looking back, but taking their hands and helping them walk forward and face the rest of their journey with less fear. That was the last time I have ever had that thought enter my mind about any of my patients—it just isn't important to the work we do.

When I first met Bob, I was surprised because he did not look sick at all. He was a very tall, large, healthy, good-looking young man who was obviously very athletic. He looked like a football player, and did play football in high school. He lived with Sharon, his high school sweetheart, whom he planned to marry someday. She was so beautiful, caring, and soft-spoken. They looked like the "perfect little couple" that you would see on a card or on television. They didn't have much; they lived in a trailer that was run down and didn't have much furniture in it, but I quickly realized that they didn't need much, just each other. They looked like they were so much in love every time they looked at each other. Even though they didn't have much as far as material things, they had more love, support, and happiness than I have seen some people have when they have all the materialistic things in the world. Their love truly did shine through all the pain, sorrow, anger, and confusion they were going through. They both had full-time jobs, and Bob was still working up until just a few weeks before that time. Sharon told me that Bob kept getting pneumonia and eye infections that were difficult to clear up and would recur all the time. He would also get bad headaches and sometimes would have small seizures. The doctors did every possible procedure and test known to medical science and could find nothing—every test, that is, except the one that no one thought to do.

This went on for months, and while the doctors continued to be baffled by Bob's condition he continued to deteriorate, leaving him and his loved ones very angry and confused about what was happening to him and wondering why they didn't have any answers. Finally, after going through several different doctors of every type of specialty and months of blood tests and procedures, Bob happened to stumble upon a doctor who had read through his history and asked him if he had ever been tested for HIV. When Bob responded that he hadn't, the doctor suggested he get tested and Bob agreed without hesitation. That little tube full of Bob's blood changed his life and everyone who loved him, forever. Sharon told me that everyone was in denial, insisting that they had mixed up the blood tubes. So, pursuant to his family's request, they took some more blood from Bob and ran the test again. As much as everyone wanted it to be a medical error, the second test also came back positive—it was no mistake. Before she had time to absorb what was happening to the man she loved, Sharon found herself in the doctor's office being tested for HIV. Her test came back negative. The doctors tested everyone and anyone who had any kind of relationship with him, including all his family and friends. Everyone's test came back negative. Bob tried some of the AIDS medication "cocktails," but only for a very short time. They were ineffective, and the doctors told him that the virus was too advanced and there was nothing that could be done. By this time Bob's condition continued to deteriorate and it had spread to his brain. His seizures were controlled by medication, but he could no longer walk and had very limited use of his arms and hands. He could not use the bathroom on his own, so he had a tube inserted into his bladder to drain the urine for him (a Foley catheter) and he had to wear diapers. Imagine having to wear diapers at twenty-six years of age, and having to have your girlfriend clean you up. When I would talk with him he was slow to respond, his speech was slurred, and he didn't always understand what I was talking about or asking him. There were times that I could tell by the look in his eyes that he did understand and had things to say but physically could not say them. I could see the frustration and sadness in him. Sometimes he had a look of fear in his eyes, probably wondering how in the world he got like this and what happened to his life. He had a lot of the same characteristics of someone with a severe brain injury or stroke. Even though he could not verbally communicate clearly, he and Sharon had an unspoken bond and she always knew what he needed and what he wanted to say. She always kept him very comfortable and clean, and made sure all his needs were met. His friends would come over and lift him out of bed into a recliner with wheels so they could push him out into the living room where they could visit and/or watch television. He had to sit straight up to eat and could no longer feed himself. Sharon would feed him most of the time, but sometimes his mother would come over and feed him. Ironically, she would sit there and feed her son just as she did twenty–five years earlier, except this time it was not the happy occasion it was many years before. She was always silent while feeding Bob, probably not knowing what to say and not really believing this was happening to her once-perfect, healthy little boy, or perhaps she just didn't have the strength to say anything. All of this had happened so fast, and with the brain involvement it was difficult to tell exactly what Bob was aware of. "I hope he isn't aware of anything because he would hate every bit of this," Sharon said. Not long after my first visit his eyes would continue to be open but he could no longer focus or track anything. The look in his eyes was empty now, no fear, no sadness, nothing. He was starting to have a difficult time swallowing, so he could only tolerate soft foods like pudding, mashed potatoes, and oatmeal, and his liquids had to be thickened up with a powdered thickener. He continued to have a good appetite, which was no surprise to anyone who knew him. Bob could no longer talk, so I got all my information from Sharon, with whom I quickly formed a bond. It would have been hard not to, because she was such a sweet, wonderful, beautiful person with unbelievable strength. She amazed me with each visit because she took such good care of him and did the majority all by herself. She could have easily just walked away but I could see the determination, love, and devotion in her eyes that she was there for the long haul. She told me once that there was never any doubt in her mind that she would care for him until the end. "It doesn't matter how or why this happened to him, what is important is that I love him and will not leave his side. He would do the same for me, that is just the kind of relationship we had." Their love was so deep and so mature for such a young couple. They were the kind of people I wish I had known before all of this happened, and would have enjoyed having as friends. Sharon continued to talk to him like she always had, even though she was unsure what he could hear or understand, if anything. She was not afraid of touching or kissing him, and continued to show him affection and love even knowing he could not give anything back.

Sharon was dealing with the whole situation better than I would have expected anyone to, especially someone so young without much life experience. I often wondered where she got her strength. How does one move on after an experience like this, even with all the strength in the world? I wonder if she has found love again? She told me that right before Bob started getting sick they were talking of getting married and were just starting to save up money for their wedding. Of course, now all the money goes towards medical bills, and she said they had accumulated thousands of dollars in medical bills. "I don't know how I will ever be able to pay all these bills, they just keep piling up," Sharon would say through tears. The entire medical bills alone must have been so overwhelming for her, then she had to deal with everything else. She seemed to be so alone in such a sad and scary world without Bob by her side. I wanted so badly to help her in some way, but just didn't know how. It broke my heart that they would never get married or have children like they had planned. He no longer had a future and her future was uncertain; she still had so much to get through. This is pain I couldn't even begin to comprehend, and I wish that no one would ever have to go through it. Young couples in love are supposed to be planning their wedding and the name of their first child, not their partner's funeral. Every time I would walk into that trailer I would carry a heavy heart for her.

They had a large group of friends who would come and visit. Most were his guy friends from high school, and some of them had been his friends since elementary school. Everyone stayed around the area after high school, so they had always remained close. I admired every one of them for their loyalty and friendship. Not one of them ran away from the situation, and no one was afraid to touch him or hug him. They were all very aware of the outcome and wanted to spend as much time with him as possible. Sometimes his friends' eyes would fill with tears when they would leave, which made my heart drop to my feet and made me wonder why they all had to be going through this. I wish I could have taken their pain away. Sharon had a few girlfriends who would come over and support her on occasion; however, she got most of her support from Bob's friends and parents. She said it was hard for her to maintain her friendships because her girlfriends didn't understand what she was going through and every time they would come over it would be very awkward because they never knew what to say or do. Her girlfriends were living different lives. They were busy getting married and having babies, something Sharon should have been doing. "I always thought that Bob and I would have our time," Sharon said with her voice shaking, holding back the tears of shattered dreams. Bob had a younger sister who did not come around at all. Sharon and she had never gotten along, and Sharon mentioned to me that she felt Bob's sister somehow blamed her for Bob getting sick. She was a very angry person and didn't want to face what was going to happen. "If she doesn't actually see it happening to her brother, then in her mind it is not happening," Sharon explained. We had no contact with her so I have no idea how she is doing or if she ever got around to facing reality.

Sharon did not have a very good family life, which did not help her out in this difficult time. She said that her whole family had recently moved out of state.

They were all aware of what she was going through but didn't "have the time" to come out and stay with her. There were numerous excuses why. Sharon told me that her parents never really approved of Bob and the lifestyle they led, "living together without being married," and her parents felt Bob held her back from going to college and broadening her horizons a little more. So, all she got was an occasional, "How are you doing?" phone call from them. Every time she would talk to me about her family she would start to cry. When I would look into her eyes I would see the little girl in her, wanting and needing her mom and dad to comfort her, wanting the innocence of childhood back where "hurts" could be fixed with a band-aid and a hug, where her mom and dad would wipe away the tears, scare away the monsters, and tell her everything would be all right. Now all grown up, Sharon was going through the most painful thing in her life and her mom and dad were not there to hold her and wipe away her tears. The worst part was that they chose not to be. She would sometimes give me a hug after our talks and thank me for listening and for all my support. This should have made me feel good, but I always walked away feeling emotionally drained. Sometimes I would feel like I was carrying some of her pain in me. "I can't believe this is happening to me," she would say, "I feel like I am dying too." All I could do was look into those pain-filled eyes, shake my head, and say, "I can't believe this is happening to you either." This was one of those moments when I knew that there were no words I could say that would express the sorrow and pain I felt for her.

I made visits out there two or three times a week, mostly to support Sharon. Bob's condition slowly declined but he never showed any signs of pain or discomfort. He never did show any of the usual signs that tell us someone is getting close to death. At the time I felt bad about not being able to educate and prepare everyone for what to expect and what was to come. Looking back on it, I'm glad Bob passed away the way he did because I don't think his loved ones who have dealt with the sometimes slow process of dying. He was only with us for about two or three months. Sharon told me that every Sunday a group of his guy friends would come over and lift him into a recliner and would sit and watch football with him. They would cheer and eat and carry on like nothing had changed from what they have been doing every Sunday. Even though Bob could not interact with them they seemed to just enjoy his physical presence. They all knew that every Sunday might be the last one they would spend with their friend. One Monday afternoon I got a call from Sharon, who said that his friends had come over and got him up in his recliner and then left. He was up for a short time when he had what Sharon thought might have been a small seizure, then he took one little gasp of breath and was gone. He was sitting straight up with his eyes wide open. She said that when she realized he was gone, she gently closed his eyes. She sounded surprisingly calm on the phone, but I did not know what lie ahead of me when I arrived at the home. When I arrived it was just Bob and Sharon. She said she wanted some time alone with him so had waited a little while before calling everyone. She said he was up most of the day the day before and watched football with his friends and seemed fine. Then when his friends came over that morning and got him up into his chair she noticed something was different about him. She told me that she could feel it in her heart that he was going to die. Right after he took his last breath, Sharon said she felt his presence all around her and described it as him giving her one last big hug and assuring her that everything would be all right. "For the first time since before he got sick, I feel like a huge weight has been lifted from me, I finally feel at peace," Sharon told me, and her eyes filled with tears.

Not long after I reached the house, his parents also arrived and then one by one his friends started coming. It was difficult to see his parents having to say good-bye to their son. How do you ever say good-bye? I don't think they ever did say good-bye, they just stood there pale with no expression to their faces, not even tears at first, just total shock and disbelief that they were staring at the lifeless body of their son. Bob's sister did not come, which did not surprise me. A few of his friends had tears rolling down their cheeks, but most of them were making this day a celebration of his life. They immediately started reminiscing about the "good old days," and then they turned their attention to supporting Sharon. It was so heartwarming and comforting to see how much love and support surrounded her. It was then for the first time I thought, "She is going to be ok." The trailer became pretty crowded; so most people went outside and congregated on the front lawn. I made my phone calls and let everyone know that the mortuary would be sending someone to pick up the body in about one hour. As I sat away from everyone and did my paperwork, I couldn't help but observe with admiration. Everyone was supporting one another and talking and laughing about "old times." I heard a lot of comments about relief for Bob because he was no longer sick and in a vegetative state. Everyone agreed that he would not like to continue to live like that. When the transport men got there, all of Bob's friends came back inside and transferred his body from the recliner onto the stretcher. I had to fight back tears watching them all transfer the lifeless body of their friend onto the gurney with such respect and love; how incredibly touching it was. Then everyone backed away and gave his parents as much time and space, as they needed to say good-bye. They each gave him a quick kiss on the forehead and said, "Good-bye son" then slowly walked away. It looked like it was in slow motion. Sharon slowly walked up to Bob's side, took his hand, and started whispering something into his ear. Even though the room was completely silent you couldn't hear what she said. It was probably something that was not meant to be heard by anyone but them. She then gently kissed his lips and walked away. It was strange to think of all the times she had kissed those lips before and now had just kissed them for the last time. His parents and Sharon gave the notice that they were done with their good-byes. His friends once again stepped up and chose to carry the gurney to the van. After the gurney was locked into place, they all stood there in a moment of silence and slowly shut the doors, knowing that was the last they would ever see of their friend, as he was to be cremated. Even though it was outside in the middle of the day, you could have heard a pin drop as the van drove away. After the van was out of sight, Bob's parents gave me a quick thank you and good-bye and were out the door. All his friends stayed. They were all standing in a circle on the front lawn, making plans to throw a party that evening in Bob's honor. I overheard them talking about what kind of food to get, who was going to get it, who was in charge of the beer, and who had to go home and change and pick up their girlfriend. While listening and watching all of this, a thought crossed my mind, "How true it is that life does go on." By then I had gathered my stuff and was talking to Sharon and letting her know I was going to leave. She gave me a hug and started to cry. When she pulled away, we locked eyes and she thanked me and I knew it was from the bottom of her heart. She said, "I'm sure Bob would want to thank you too." So she gave me another hug and said that that one was from Bob. She held on a little tighter this time and didn't want to let go, and I wondered if in some strange way she thought by letting go of me she was letting go of Bob. She finally pulled away, and as I looked at her, even though she was younger than I was, she seemed so much older and wiser. Then I realized she was in a sense so much older, wiser, and stronger than I could ever be. She had just gone through an experience that made her grow up way before her time. She had just gone through something most people don't experience until much later in life, after they have lots of life experiences behind them and not in front of them. She did it with such dignity and courage. She wiped her tears and assured me she would be all right. "I am very lucky, I have all of them," she said as she pointed outside to the large circle of friends Bob had left behind. There were about eight or ten of them, and every one of them had promised Bob to look after Sharon and help her through this. There was no doubt in my mind that they would carry out their promise.

As I started walking across the street to my car, I heard numerous thank-you's from all his friends and I turned and waved back, not really knowing what to say.

Feeling awkward again and realizing that we were all around the same age. I sat in my car and finished up my paperwork when I suddenly noticed that my paper was getting wet. It took me a few seconds to realize that it was from my tears. It was a very surreal experience because I was so emotionally drained by the whole situation that I was crying without feeling emotions. As I glanced over to "the group" I had flashes of my group of friends and started thinking about each one of them and how they would react in a situation like this. How would I react if it was me standing out there after saying good-bye to a friend? That's when it hit a little too close to home and my heart skipped a beat and for a second I could not catch my breath. I wiped away my tears and tried to collect myself but all I wanted to do was go home and call all my friends and make sure they were ok. I then remembered I still had one more visit to make but I knew I couldn't do it. The only thing I could focus on was wanting every single one of my friends with me at that moment. I called my supervisor and she was very supportive, just like she said she would be. She told me to go home and that she would call my other patient and see if she could reschedule the visit for tomorrow, if not she said she would go out herself. I found myself crying most of the way home, and not for one particular reason. There were just so many things going through my head, some of them made my heart ache, and some made me feel relieved that it was over for everyone involved and that Bob was at peace. I felt so drained I guess a part of me just didn't know what else to do. I felt a little better once I got home but I no longer wanted to talk to anyone, I wanted to grieve this one alone. I remember spending a lot of quiet time alone that night just reflecting on young love, true friendships, family, life and love in general.

This was a "reality check" for me. It really brought home the facts that no one is immune from getting a terminal illness, and that we can die at any age. Life can change so incredibly quickly and then be gone in an instant. I saw first hand the power of friendship and how a situation like this one can make you grow up far beyond your years. True friends are there until the end, and Bob was lucky enough to have a large group of true friends who in my eyes are better people because of what they did for their friend.

# Needing Space

Part of being a home hospice nurse is that sometimes you have to take call at night. Every time the pager goes off, you jump up out of a sound sleep and wonder if you are going to have to go out. It was my turn to be on call, and the pager went off around 1:00 A.M. or so. There was a frantic family member on the other end of the phone stating that her grandfather was very agitated and the family could not calm him down. I tried to talk to her over the phone and get more information so I could tell her what to do, but she was too upset and requested to have a nurse come out. This was not one of my patients so I knew very little about the patient or family. So I had no idea what I was walking into. I threw myself together the best I could at 1:00 A.M. and still look professional. I tried to wake myself up before hitting the road. Looking at the address, I realized I had a good thirty-to forty-minute drive, which would give me plenty of time to wake up.

I drove up to this house where there were cars and people everywhere. At first I thought I had the wrong house because it looked like a big party. I checked the address about three times and it was the house. It was a tiny brick house at the end of a road. I cautiously started walking up to the house when the granddaughter I had spoken with on the phone greeted me and she led me into the house. Not far behind were a number of people that were outside who followed us in. The house inside was full of people too. I could not believe how many people there were, and they were all family. There must have been at least three or four generations there. After making my way through the crowd, as if I was in a bar, I finally got to a little bedroom where the patient was, and wouldn't you know it, inside the bedroom were more people. I couldn't even see the patient; there were people on the bed, around the bed, everywhere. The granddaughter and another family member took charge and told everyone to get out so I could assess him. Finally, the last few reluctantly got off the bed and left the room. The crowd did not go far though, as many as possible stood in the doorway, I could feel numerous pairs of eyes staring at me. I was a little nervous knowing that whatever my assessment of the patient was I was going to have to tell all these people. I finally got to see the patient, who was a tiny, elderly man lying on a twin bed. He was visibly agitated, and looked scared. His blood pressure and pulse were really low despite all the agitation and commotion. He was semi-responsive and unable to communicate. After my assessment I knew that this patient did not have long to live, I was guessing another couple of days. When people are close to death they get a glassy look to their eyes, and this man had that look. I asked the family if they had given him any Ativan (an antianxiety medication we use to calm people down) and the said they had about thirty minutes before but it didn't work. It was so hot and stuffy in that room that I was even starting to get agitated. After assessing the patient I asked everyone to go out into the other room so we could all talk and the patient could have some time to rest. They did, but they left the bedroom door open and there were so many people that some were still standing in the doorway. All eyes were on me, eagerly awaiting what I had to say, and that was a lot of eyes! I knew I had to be honest with this family and wasn't sure how they would react. So, I took a deep breath and thought to myself, "Here it goes." I started explaining to the family that based on my assessment the patient's condition, he was rapidly declining and he probably only had a couple of days or so left to live. His agitation was coming from getting too much stimulation, such as people on the bed, others constantly stroking him, talking, stuffiness of the room, and all the commotion. He could also be having what we call "terminal agitation," which happens to some patients when death nears and they know it is getting closer and they get scared. A lot of commotion can sometimes make this worse. When patients get this close to dying some need a quiet, calm environment and need their space to be alone. I suggested to the granddaughter that he get some more Ativan right now and some Roxanol (liquid Morphine) in case he was in pain. This man looked so uncomfortable and I knew that he was going to need a lot more medication than he had been getting to make him comfortable. I just hoped the family would give it to him. Sometimes when people are really agitated it can also be a sign of pain, so it's good to medicate for both agitation and pain. She agreed and went to medicate him. A lot of the family members admitted that they did not want him to die, so they would sit on his bed and when he would fall asleep or start "breathing funny" they would shake him awake and/or jump on the bed to make sure he was still alive. Even if you weren't dying this would make you agitated. I strongly, but subtly, suggested that they not shake him at all, explaining to them that when they did that it obviously scared him and made him agitated. This man was trying to die in peace, but his family would not let him. When people are in the "actively dying" stage, meaning they could die within days or hours, they can actually be starting their journey and the family can pull them back by shaking them or jumping on the bed, which is very distressing to the patient. I tried to explain that to the family and encouraged them to respect his wishes to die in peace.

I told the family that I realize no one is ever ready for their loved one to die but that it was important to let him know he is loved, that everything and everyone will be fine, and give him permission to go on his journey. I explained that although this is not easy for anyone to do, it would ease some of his agitation. Sometimes the agitation comes from the patient not wanting to leave all their loved ones. This is difficult on the loved ones too, but the patient needs to hear that if they are ready to go their need will be respected. As I looked around the room, some family members started crying, others looked like they finally realized what was happening, and others looked at me like I was completely nuts. I left instructions for the family to continue to medicate him until he looked comfortable. I told them that he should look like he is in a peaceful sleep all the time. I strongly recommended that only two people go into his room at a time and stay for a short while, then rotate. I also told them not to shake the bed or shake him. I said that holding his hand and gently talking with him is was fine. Some family members had some questions, which I took the time to answer, and before leaving I made sure no one had any more questions and everyone understood what I had been talking about. I knew there were some people who didn't listen to a word I said, and I could tell by the faces of some family members that they didn't believe a word I said. Some didn't even come in from outside. I realized that I can't educate those who don't want to be educated or involved. I just hope I reached at least one of them or more. I wrote down a summary of everything and how he should be medicated so everyone could have directions to which to refer.

I also prepared the family that some people want to die alone. Dying is a very private thing for some and they don't want anyone in the room with them. Others want everyone surrounding them. So, I let them know that they needed to give him some space and time alone, and not to feel guilty in any way if they were not with him when he died. I said that everyone needs to just go about their business, but to still check on him regularly and make sure he is comfortable. I also told them that it was not necessary to sit in there staring at him, not wanting to even blink for fear of feeling they wouldn't be there when he died. I said that if he wanted someone or everyone with him when he died, he would make sure that happens, but that if he wanted to die alone, he would find the opportunity and just slip away. By this point I had almost all of them crying, which I felt badly about, but I felt they needed to know this information ahead of time. I have found that most families are able to deal with things a lot better if they have been educated about what to expect before it happens.

I finally starting making my way back through the crowd to my car. Most of the family members thanked me for coming out and answering all their questions. When I stepped outside, the fresh air felt so good. That house was so crowded and stuffy. As I drove home I wasn't totally convinced that they would follow any of my instructions. I felt so badly for the patient, and hoped that his family would allow him to die a peaceful, comfortable death. I did all I could; it was up to them now. I got home and was so exhausted went right back to sleep. The pager went off about two hours later but to me it seemed like thirty minutes. It was a different family member but the same family. In my mind I thought, "Now what? Please don't tell me I have to go down there again." Then when I heard that the patient had died I felt really badly for thinking that. I was not expecting this to happen. I was shocked that he had died so soon and wondered how the family was dealing with it. So, I got up and threw on the same clothes and was off and running again. I arrived again at the house and there seemed to be fewer people there, which surprised me. There was no longer anyone outside and inside there were just a few people sitting around. The same granddaughter I had communicated with the first time showed me to the patient's room. She tearfully said that he was completely alone when he died. She let me know that everyone listened to my instructions, although some of them were difficult for her to convince. Some chose to leave without saying good-bye; a choice they will have to live with. Eventually everyone who was still there was in agreement and they all took turns going into the room and saying good-bye and anything else they wanted to say, then let the next person go in. After everyone was through, the granddaughter went to get some Ativan and Roxanol for him to make sure he was comfortable. As she walked into the room with his medications she noticed he was no longer breathing. She closed the door, afraid that some of the family members would still try to shake him, and she did not want that. She called hospice from his room and then she said she sat in there with him, just holding his hand. No one disturbed her until they knocked on the door to tell her that I had arrived. The family was grieving appropriately, some crying harder than others were, but overall I felt it went pretty well. A couple of family members came up to me and were totally amazed that what I had told them was right. I felt so happy and relieved for the patient, because he finally got the space and peace of mind he needed to let go.

Sometimes it is so difficult to educate families about their loved one dying, answering the most difficult questions, and trying to teach them about a difficult subject at such a painful and frightening time in their lives. Knowing you can't take their pain away makes you feel helpless, but making sure they are educated and as prepared as one could be makes you feel a little better. The reward comes after you see that the families actually listened to you and followed your instructions and advice; and they saw that what you told them actually worked. It truly warms your heart because you know that you have just helped someone die comfortably and with peace of mind that they would not have had otherwise. It also allows the family to be prepared for and educated about the dying process and death. I felt very proud about all the work I did with this large family, not even knowing until the end whether any of it made a difference. I knew I had to do it anyway, not just for the family but for the patient too. The patient who could no longer verbalize his needs and wants needed me to be his voice.

# A Hard Road

Not everyone has an easy transition at the end of his or her life. A couple of years ago I was working in a hospice facility and there was a young man who was admitted. He was only about forty, but had obviously made some bad choices and led a hard life. He was dying because his liver was failing due to all the hard alcohol and drug abuse he had done. His arms were filled with scars where he would shoot the drugs into his bloodstream; he even had some on his feet because all the veins in his arms were ruined. His stomach was very large and his skin was yellow. These symptoms the result of the liver not functioning correctly to remove fluid and toxins from the body. He was not a pleasant man. I don't know if that was who he was or who he became because of his lifestyle. Also, with a diagnosis like this sometimes your whole body becomes very toxic, including your brain, which leads to behavioral changes. He was always cussing and yelling at someone, and sometimes he would sit in his room alone and yell and carry on conversations with no one. He would sometimes see or feel things, usually bugs, crawling on him. The facility had to keep him in a room by himself because his behavior was so unpredictable no one knew what he would do from one minute to the next. There were many days that I would walk into his room and find that he had thrown his food tray across the room or urinated on the floor. He would always completely destroy his bed and get all tangled up in the sheets and refuse to have anyone help him; he did not like the bed made up. A lot of times he would be in the middle of his bed, the sheets all torn apart, and he would cover his head with them and have his butt sticking straight up in the air. He was not fond of keeping clothes on either. He would spit out his medications that were meant to calm him. Getting medication into him was very tricky, and most days impossible. This man was obviously uncomfortable physically, emotionally, and spiritually, but he refused the support and care available to him. Once in a while he would be very cooperative and nice, but everyone who entered that room kept their guard up because his mood could change in a blink of an eye. The man scared me but I knew that he needed and deserved the same care everyone else did. No one knows how much of his behavior was him or his toxic body. I would sometimes watch him from the doorway before going in to see what kind of mood he was in. I watched him do some very bizarre things that I knew any sane person of sound mind would not do. This led me to believe that most, if not all, of his behaviors were disease-related or possibly due to the withdrawal from constantly having a high level of drugs and alcohol in his bloodstream.

He was with us for about three or four months, and not once did I see or hear of anyone coming to see him. I knew from his chart that he was divorced and had children, siblings, and parents. It must have been so difficult for those who loved him to watch him destroy himself with drugs and alcohol, knowing there is so much help out there for these addictions but he refused to take it. After about a month of constantly fighting us he slowly started to calm down. I think he wore himself out from putting up such a fight constantly for so long. I got tired just watching him. It was amazing how he was in constant motion for weeks with very little sleep and little food or fluids because he preferred to throw them across the room. After he started letting us medicate him he was much calmer. He was very paranoid, though, and would always question what we were giving him, to make sure he wasn't being poisoned. He would even pick apart his food thinking we put the poison in there and then would throw it across the room. He wasn't taking any chances just in case we had "poisoned" the food. He always thought someone was out to get him. Over time his skin became more yellow and he lost weight everywhere but his stomach. He was too weak to walk any more, and had to wear adult diapers, which some days he would tear up into little pieces and they would be everywhere. Even though I saw a lot of fear and sadness in his eyes, it was difficult for me to feel sympathetic towards him; after all, he did this to himself. But on the other hand I had to realize that there must have been something that made him choose this destructive path. I had to constantly remind myself not to judge him because I had not walked in his shoes. As open-minded and nonjudgmental as I tried to be, some days were very difficult and nearly impossible. As his condition declined more he started having pain and a lot of anxiety. He would yell out a lot, most of the time in incomprehensible language. His eyes were as big as saucers all the time; the man was scared and uncomfortable. I made numerous calls to the doctor to get his medications changed and/or increased. This patient was challenging because his symptoms were so out of control and nothing seemed to be working. It was always such a fight to get anything into him on a regular basis. We finally found a combination of high doses of morphine and Ativan that worked. This man was medicated every hour, and it took at least twenty-four hours before we saw the medicine starting to work. The medicine was given under his tongue or between his gum and cheek so he didn't even have to be aware of it, which is good because once he was calm no one wanted to disturb him. He did not have to swallow the medication because it absorbs into the membranes. I never saw him close his eyes; they were always wide open but their was no response in them, just fear. His breathing had become labored so he was put on oxygen and amazingly he kept it on, most of the time anyway. I could tell by looking at him that he had very little fight left in him. Even with all the medication we were giving him, he would constantly moan. Every day I would come back to work and the night shift would say that he moaned all night. A chaplain had been in there to talk with him—nothing. The social worker tried to contact some of his family; the ones she reached were not interested in coming, and some she couldn't locate. His constant moaning went on for at least four or five days straight; the medication was increased but didn't stop the moaning.

One day when I walked into work, I made it my personal mission to get this man comfortable. I called the doctor and got the medications increased again; I could not believe how much he was getting and still moaning, let alone still breathing. The doctor decided to add a third medication, an antipsychotic drug. So every hour I would go in there and give him as much medication as I could per doctor's orders. His eyes continued to be open and I rarely saw him blink; it was a fixed stare. I could still see the fear and sadness in his eyes and when I would walk into the room there was such bad energy, it was very creepy—the kind of feeling that makes your hair stand up on the back of your neck, and gives you chills. I knew this man probably had so many regrets and unresolved issues that would now have to stay unresolved. He was dying and he was alone because of the choices he had made and the way he had treated others. Halfway through my shift I was completely out of ideas and mentally exhausted. I had no idea how to give this man some sort of peace. Regardless of what he had done, I did not want him to die this way. I was very uncomfortable every time I went into his room because it was filled with such bad energy. His eyes felt like they were burning right through me, especially when I walked away. Even though there was fear, I also saw a little part of him deep down inside screaming, "Please help me!" Every hair on my body would be standing on end when I would look at him. Being in the room actually gave me chills. It always felt so cold in only his room and not temperature cold, it was much more.

After my lunch break I walked by his room and the door was closed. I asked another nurse why his door was closed and she said that his ex-wife was in there. I didn't want to disturb them. I kept an eye on the door so I would know when she came out in case she wanted to talk. She was in there for about fifteen or twenty minutes when I saw her walk out and close the door. She stood at the door and looked around and I could tell she was looking for someone to talk to. I walked up to her and introduced myself as his nurse and I could see she had been crying and tears were still running down her face. She asked me how long he had and I told her he probably only had a couple days at the most. She said she had no idea his condition was this bad, and no one had informed her until a couple of days before that he was in hospice dying. She started telling me about their life together and how difficult it was for her to put up with the drug and alcohol abuse and the behavior that went with it. His family had completely abandoned him, so she was all he had. She said that she kicked him out soon after their second son was born because she didn't want them growing up in that kind of environment. She said she tried to move on with her two sons, but confessed that she took him back a couple of times because he was homeless. She said he would show up at her front door late at night looking very dirty, sick, and hungry with no place to go. "I couldn't shut the door on him," She said. He would always promise her that things would get better, but refused to get treatment. He was in and out of hospitals and jail numerous times and she would always go get him and take care of him for a while until things would get so bad she would have to throw him out again. She started to cry and said, "He was doing so well for awhile and I thought things were going to get better. I had forgiven him and we were going to work things out. Then one night about six months ago he just got up and left the kids and me. I had no idea were he went and I never heard from him again. When I called around no one had heard from him; it was like he had vanished. The next thing I know I get a phone call at work from his sister who told me he was in hospice dying. She was still crying but trying to be strong. "How can he be dying?" she asked me. I gave her a hug and she said she was going to go because it was too difficult for her. "It's so hard to see him like this. He has changed so much. I have always loved him so much." She told me she wasn't going to come back, even when he died.

She would now have to find the strength to deal with the unresolved issues between them, his death, and her love for him. I escorted her down the hallway, thinking of how sad the whole situation was and realizing how destructive drugs and alcohol were. They not only destroy the person using but they destroy everyone's lives that love them, and I saw that in her eyes. Her life and the lives of everyone who loved him had been forever scarred because of his choices. I watched her walk across the parking lot with her head hung down, crying. Then I went back down the hallway and opened up the door to his room and noticed for the first time his eyes were closed, and I saw that he was taking his last few breaths. I went to get my stethoscope and by the time I came back he was gone.

He had such a peaceful look on his face. I saw no more fear or sadness. The energy in the room was no longer eerie, but peaceful. I let out a big sigh of relief because he finally looked comfortable and all the bad energy was gone. It all came together in my mind that he was waiting for her, and on some level he knew she would come. I often wonder what she said to him in there but then realize that doesn't matter. What matters is that it gave him what he needed to let go. He struggled so much and was so uncomfortable and scared. It felt so good to look at him knowing he was no longer suffering. It's amazing to see the power of the human spirit and how it needs love, understanding, and forgiveness, and how the love and soulful connection between two people is so strong that it has the power for one of them to be able to somehow set the other one free from their suffering so they may begin their journey. I now realize that no amount of medication could ever be that powerful.

I struggled to find meaning to this man's struggle. I then realized that it was quite simple. Everyone has a heart, and they need to feel love and forgiveness. Even when they have, for whatever reasons, turned down the wrong road, they need to have the comfort of knowing that at the end the ones they love and who once loved them will be there. Before your soul can go on it must be set free from regrets and made aware that everyone will be fine when you are gone. I definitely learned that there is no medication or technology that will calm a person with a soul filled with emotional distress and regret; they need resolution, forgiveness, and love.

# Mr. Irish

Patrick was an Irish gentleman I took care of for only about four months but it seemed like I had known him a lot longer. He had been with hospice for a while when I took over his care because his original nurse was moving out of state. He was not exactly open to the idea of getting a new nurse and then when he found out his new nurse was also young, he really objected. At first he flat out refused, stating he wanted an "older nurse." It took a couple phone calls from my supervisor explaining to him that the only nurse available to care for him was a younger nurse, which happened to be me. After some hesitation he reluctantly agreed. I knew even before I met him that I had to go in to his home with a lot of confidence, be prepared to meet resistance and somehow win him over. When I first met him he made it obvious that he was not happy about the situation, which I expected. Our first few visits were very short. He did not want to talk to me any more than he had to, and would only give me "yes" and "no" answers and would become very angry when he could not hear me. "Ma'am!" he would shout at me when he did not hear me. I learned that I had to speak in a raised, clear voice and speak directly to him in order for him to hear and understand me. Sometimes he would get angry with me for asking what, in his mind, was the wrong question. I would ask him, "How is your breathing today?" which is a standard question asked of anyone who has a difficult time breathing and is dependent on oxygen. I was looking for a response of either it is better or worse than last week. Well, his reply would always be, "My breathing is the same, ma'am. It never changes, and that is why I can't do anything!" I quickly learned not to ask that question. He did better when he wasn't asked any questions at all. I learned it was better to let him speak on his own and to let him tell me only the information he felt I needed to know, no more and no less. Of course, I still tried to get more information sometimes but learned that it was a waste of time because he would always refuse to answer. This left me feeling like I was only able to do half my job and get half the information I usually do. But realized I had to let some things go, and to just focus on whether he was comfortable and safe and forget about the details. I learned to let a lot of details go with Patrick. I always made sure he was safe and comfortable and knew that if he weren't comfortable he would have no problem letting me know. He never appeared to be in any pain or distress and was very content with where he was. At first I didn't exactly look forward to our visits because he was so closed off and I felt like I was walking on eggshells, never knowing if what I would say or do would make him angry. I continued to be very patient with him, gave him space, and let him "run the show," and after awhile he started to relax with me a little bit. He started to make conversation with me and when he found out that I was Irish all the tension and doubt within him fell away. From that moment on we got along just fine and I learned what to say and what not to say, which helped too.

He lived alone in this tiny little apartment. His wife died of cancer almost ten years before. They had three children, and his eldest son died in an accident when he was in his early twenties. His two living children lived in town but did not come around much; mostly on the weekends or whenever they had time. They did not seem to want to be too involved in what was happening to their father, or maybe he didn't want them to be. I would leave them notes after my visits to encourage them to write me with any questions or call me, but the whole time I took care of him I heard nothing. Patrick would always sit in a recliner that seemed to swallow him up because he was nothing but skin and bones. The recliner was of normal size, but it looked huge when you saw this tiny little man sitting in it. His whole apartment was decorated with Irish sayings and sham-rocks. He had bookshelves full of books on Ireland and picture albums of his trips there. There were big Irish beer mugs and little knickknacks all over. It smelled of strong, stale cigarette smoke, which I got used to after a while. He lived on the ground level so it was always really dark and gloomy in there. The more closely I looked at him the more I realized he actually looked like a lepre-chaun. He was suffering from lung cancer and was dependent on oxygen. Of course, he would still smoke with his oxygen on and refused to believe that it was flammable. I am amazed that he did not catch himself on fire or burn the whole apartment complex down. He did respect his guests, however, and never smoked in front of anyone who was in his home. He was short of breath all the time, and even talking would make it worse, but he was determined to tell stories. He loved to tell stories of Ireland and growing up in Denver and how the world has changed. I could have listened to him forever because I found everything he said so fascinating, but his stories were always cut short because if he talked too long he would start coughing and he would become too short of breath to continue, then I knew it was time for me to go.

When he was in a good mood and his breathing was ok, he loved having com-pany, so we would sit there and look at books of Ireland and he would show me pictures of his trips to Ireland and tell me stories. I saw him every Monday morning, he was my first patient, and I looked forward to it. It was a nice way to start the week off, and I always allowed extra time between him and my next visit so that I could spend extra time with him. I always thought that he needed more than one nurse visit a week because he lived alone but he wouldn't hear of it. "There are other patients that need you more than me," he would say. And since he was very much alert and oriented he had the right to refuse, so I kept my visits to once a week. I could tell that he liked his time alone, although once in a while he would mention that he was lonely and thought about going to an inpatient facility to be around people. That idea never lasted long because he would realize he wanted to stay in his home and die there. He had a screen glass door with a little patio that he could see from his chair. He would feed the squirrels that would come around. They always got peanuts, and he had names for all of them. If the screen door was not kept closed the squirrels would walk right into his house and start begging for food. He said that he really enjoyed looking out the patio door and watching the squirrels and whatever other activity was going on outside. "It is my only link to the outside world now," he would say. "I haven't been out of this apartment for about three years."

For the most part Patrick was a pretty serious man, and very stubborn. But as time went on I could tell that he looked forward to my visits and would greet me as I walked in the door with a big smile and a "Hi punkin." Our relationship had come a long way and that made me feel really good. Seeing him then warmed my heart. My goal for each visit was to get him to laugh or even just smile which I succeeded in doing most days. If I didn't I knew he was really having a difficult time breathing but that didn't happen very often. He didn't have many teeth left so when he smiled it was a grin of mostly gums. It really made me feel good to make him smile, and I would unintentionally make him laugh every time I would leave because I could never get his screen door to close easily, so I would have to stand there and fight with it, seeing him grinning at me the whole time. "You are the only person that has trouble with that door," he would laugh through the screen. That door always gave me trouble, but it was worth the frustration because it made him laugh.

Patrick was very Catholic and every time I would come for my visit he would say that he had been praying and saying "Hail Mary's" all the time and couldn't understand why he was still alive. This man was ready to die the day I met him, but for some reason it wasn't his time. "I must still have something to do," he would say. "But I don't know what because I have lived a good life and have no regrets." Not knowing why he woke up every morning bothered him more than being sick. He no longer ate anything, and would only drink Ensure supplements. I didn't think it was possible for him to get any thinner, but he did. His skin was actually transparent and a small child's blood pressure cuff could wrap around his arm twice and still be a little too big. Amazingly, his blood pressure and pulse were always pretty good. He was too weak to walk far, only to the bathroom on occasion. We had good conversations and he would make me laugh. He didn't talk about his family much, which surprised me, but I knew not to push. Every time I would start to leave he would say, "May the Lord keep you in the palm of his hand, be careful out there punkin, and have a good day." My heart would just melt everytime he would call me punkin. It was in the way he said it, so caring, and about someone he didn't really know, only saw once a week, whom he didn't exactly welcome into his home and his life at first. He admitted that in his life he had done some "wrong things" and gotten into trouble a lot for a while, but deep down I could tell that this man had a big heart.

Every week he would look a little worse, a little thinner, which I didn't think was possible. When I would leave I always wondered if that would be the last time I would see him. In my mind, I knew that he could die at any time because his lungs were barely working. When I would listen to them with my stethoscope it was like listening to a wall, and usually I heard air going through them. One Monday during one of my visits he shared with me that September 29th was the day his wife, father, and mother-in-law all died, only in different years. He hinted, and hoped, that maybe that would be his day. In my mind I was actually hoping it would be because I knew how ready he was to die. When I left that day I told him I would see him next week and for the first time he said, "I will either be here or six feet under at the cemetery," and he gave out a little nervous laugh after having said that. Since he had never said that before, I thought that maybe he would die that day or before. Well, that day came and went and he was still living and continuing to wonder why, and so was I. He never really showed any signs of his condition declining, and when I would check him over everything was pretty much the same week after week. He looked very sick, but nothing changed in his outward appearance. Of course, I don't think it was possible for him to look any sicker anyway. He asked me a couple of weeks later what would happen to him if he were to fall and hit his head in the bathroom. He refused to wear any kind of lifeline so that he could push a button for help. I asked him how often someone checked on him, and he said one of his children called every day, usually several times. I reassured him that if he didn't answer like he usually did, his children would come check on him. After talking he seemed to be reassured, but I thought it was a strange conversation because he had never shown concern about things like that before. I asked him if he had fallen in the bathroom and he said no. I knew of a couple times he had fallen in the living room—once his son was there and the other time he was able to pull himself back up. He told me that his birthday was October 20$^{th}$ and said emphatically that he did not want anything done for him and he did not want anyone, including his children, to get him anything. His birthday happened to fall on a Monday, my visit day, and for a second I did think of bringing him something but thought I better respect his wishes. Besides, what do you give someone for their last birthday?

The Monday before his birthday I had a nursing student with me, so we were unable to have our usual conversation and laughs. Plus, he did not do well with more than one person in his house at a time. "It's too much and I can't breathe," he would say. So, he was pretty quiet throughout the visit, but physically doing the same. Thinking back, it was very strange because that day when I left with the nursing student, for the first time since I have taken care of him, it never entered my mind that that would be the last time I would see him. Usually after each visit I would walk to my car wondering and trying to prepare myself for the chance that I had just seen him alive for the last time, and I always thought that he would die in the night and the social worker or I would find him in the morning and have to notify the family. Almost every day I wondered when I would receive that call to notify me that he had died or that he could no longer stay at home and had to be transferred to an inpatient facility, but weeks went by and I heard nothing. Every Monday I would be truly amazed that he was still alive. Monday, October 20$^{th}$ came around, and I stopped by the office to pick up some paperwork. I was looking forward to going to visit him. I wanted to wish him a happy birthday and I was looking forward to our usual conversation since we didn't have one the previous week. Right before I left, my supervisor asked me if I knew that he had passed away over the weekend. I was shocked, but on the other hand not really surprised. I was so relieved for him; he finally got his wish. All those "Hail Mary's" finally paid off for him. As I talked with my supervisor, I inquired about the circumstances of his death and how the family was doing. My supervisor proceeded to tell me that he had fallen in the bathroom and hit his head, just like he was afraid of. My mind immediately went back to the conversation we had just weeks before about his fear of that happening. I suddenly got the chills and found that very strange. Had he predicted his own death? Someone called 911 and he ended up in one hospital then was transferred to another where he died a short time later. I asked who had called 911, and my supervisor didn't know. I asked the nurses that worked over the weekend when it happened and no one knew who called 911. A short time later I talked with his nurse practitioner and asked her if she knew who had found him. She said she didn't know, but did know that it was not his children because they were notified by the hospital, as was she. My mind was going ninety miles an hour, wondering who else was there. He was so thin that neighbors would not have heard him fall, and if he was knocked unconscious he couldn't have done it and even if he was awake he couldn't reach the phone. The mystery of who called 911 remains unsolved, and the whole circumstances surrounding his death are very eerie to me.

There was a selfish part of me that was upset because I did not get to say good-bye, and my last visit with him was not the way I wanted it to be. Even though I have done this type of work for so long, every once in a while I find my human emotions coming out with some patients more than others. After all, we are human too, and we hurt and grieve just like everyone else, no matter how much we try to hold it in, and no matter how long we have been doing hospice work. The way he died upset me more than him dying because I knew he did not want to die like that. We had talked about it several times. He wanted to die in his recliner, in his home. I remember him having me tape his Do Not Resuscitate paper, the hospice number, and his living will stating his wishes all on the wall right in front of his recliner. He wanted to make sure they were in plain sight for all to see and could readily be seen from the screen door. I hope he was not frightened when all of this happened to him. Not knowing the details was difficult for me because when hospice patients die we almost always know every detail of what happened leading up to their death or we are lucky enough to say good-bye at the death.

I left the office and went about my day, having him in the back of my mind and wishing so badly that I could have told him good-bye or been there with him. I wish his life hadn't ended like that, but as I have said in my other stories, if he wanted me there I would have been there, and if he wanted a chance to say good-bye to me he would have. I got through my day, but I didn't really feel very well. It wasn't until after I got home and started writing this story that the tears started to fall. I realized that I would never see him again, and would never make him laugh or hear anymore of his stories. I felt like he still had so much to tell. I will miss him, and my Monday mornings won't be as cheerful. There will be no more, "See ya later punkin, be careful out there and have a good day." This voice will now remain silent forever.

Patrick was one of those patients who seemed to have lived with no regrets and was very ready to die, but for some reason did not for a long time. There are sometimes reasons that no one understands that someone so ill and so ready to die still has lessons to learn or things to teach before their soul is ready. It is amazing when you examine someone like Patrick and physically there is no explanation how the body could possibly still be functioning. No matter how hard he prayed and how long he went without eating or drinking there was something left for him to do here, and it wasn't until all was resolved within him that his physical body would let go.

In his memory, here are a few of his favorite Irish sayings of which I have become fond as well.

May the road rise to meet you, may the wind be always at your back.

May you live as long as you want and never want as long as you live.

May your right hand always be stretched out in friendship and never in want.

And lastly, may your heart be warm and happy with the lilt of Irish laughter, every day in every way and forever and ever after.

I hope in some way he knew how he brightened my days and touched me. May my little Mr. Irish finally rest in peace.

# Iris's Journey

With this next story I would like to invite you to come with me on a journey as I care for an extraordinary person through her illness and the end of her life. She wanted her story to be told in the hope that it would help others face their terminal illness with a little less fear. She strongly believed in hospice care and all the support it gave both the patients and their loved ones. She wanted everyone to know about it, and every chance she got she educated anyone who would listen that hospice was, "...not about dying, it was about living comfortably until it's time for you to die." She was proud to be a hospice patient. She told me that being in hospice made her feel special, secure, and not so alone. Because she did live by herself, she said it was comforting for her to know that at any time she could pick up the phone and hospice would be there for her. Hospice was there to answer all her questions because she wanted to know everything that was going on and what was going to happen. She was not afraid of death or what lie ahead for her. "Everyone must die from something, it is the normal progression of things. And after all, your body is just the shell of who you really are, and your soul goes on to live forever." Iris would always tell me that, as a society, people needed to stop fearing death so much. "There's nothing to be afraid of," she would say.

I did not know her before her illness but she would tell me stories here and there. She actually did not talk about her family much. I don't know why and felt it was not my business to know. I do know that she was married twice and her second husband was the love of her life, Bob. She talked about their life together a lot and how much fun they had together. Iris lost Bob three years before to lung cancer. He had died peacefully in their home, with hospice care, as she sat at his bedside. She had grown children, grandchildren, and great grandchildren. I never met or talked with any of them except her son, right before her death. She was born and grew up in Denver, her siblings lived in other states but she was not close to them. She and Bob used to love to square dance, and they were really into antique shopping. She had given me a medical dictionary from 1903. We sat there together looking through it and laughing at the pictures and some of the stuff they used back then (no wonder people died young). The thing that really made us laugh was the way they used to do CPR by pumping someone's arms up and down over their head. It really meant a lot to me that she wanted me to have that. Iris was always trying to talk me into trying square dancing or something else that I would never consider doing. I would laugh and kindly say, "I don't think so." As hard as she tried she was unsuccessful. "That's ok," she said. "The important thing is for you to pick something that you enjoy and go out and have fun." She never liked it when she would ask me what I had done for the past week and I would say "Nothing." Part of that was me trying to keep somewhat of a professional relationship with her. I remember being taught not to tell your patients too much about your personal life, they have enough to worry about. This time is about them, their life and loved ones, not you.

As I got to know her I began to feel incredibly honored to be her nurse and to have the moments we did each week sitting at the table talking and laughing. Those will always be truly treasured memories for me. She willingly and openly allowed me into her life and her thoughts as she faced her illness and her death. She allowed me to ask any question and she would tell me anything. Everything she went through she did with incredible courage and strength. I feel privileged that she allowed me to be by her side. Sometimes I don't know who helped whom more through this. I think we were there for each other in different ways and for different reasons. I was there to help her through the end of her life and she was there for me to teach me how to live life. Her amazing spirit, calming peace, and sense of humor are qualities I will not forget. She was someone truly special who will always have a special place in my heart.

I met Iris in July of 2003. She had been in hospice for five months already. She was under the care of another nurse when I had started with the company. Her nurse was caring for too many patients at the time so they gave Iris to me. Iris was seventy-one and had emphysema and lung disease, called COPD (chronic-obstructive-pulmonary-disease). She was a long-time smoker, and still smoked at times. She was on oxygen all the time and got short of breath whenever she would do too many activities. Since her late husband had hospice care she knew what to expect. I remember the first time I called her to introduce myself and make an appointment to come out to see her. I gave her a time that worked with my schedule, and she said, "I don't know if that will work or not. You need to know that I am very hard to get along with," and started laughing. I was not quite sure what to think of that response.

I never would have imagined that with that one phone call, my life would be changed forever. When I met her we hit it off right away and I knew that we would get along just fine. She was rarely, if ever, serious about anything. We had the same sense of humor, so I thought she was hilarious and she constantly had me laughing. Physically she looked pretty good. If not for the oxygen tubing it would be very difficult to tell she was even sick just by looking at her. Her breathing was ok unless she really exerted herself. She would drag the oxygen tubing around behind her like a leash. I never heard her once complain of having to wear oxygen. Now that I think about it she never really complained at all. When I would visit she would go through the kitchen, and I would go through the living room and we would meet in the middle at a small dining room table. She was worried that one of us would get tripped up on the oxygen cord. It took me a couple of visits, but then I had the routine down. She had one of those electric chairs that went up and down the stairs, and she was always asking me if I wanted "to take it for a ride." I declined because she had steep stairs and it looked too scary for me. "It's like an amusement ride, it's fun, so if you ever think of anyone that would like to try it, bring them by." All I could do was laugh and think to myself, "I can't believe she just said that." Of course, I did not know her very well yet so had no idea that there was much more comments like that to come. I could tell that she was going to be around for a while, unless she took a sudden decline. Patients with lung disorders are difficult to predict. Sometimes they can last years, other times a few months to a few weeks. Even though she only had two teeth left, both on the bottom with a big space in between, her smile could still light up a room. She would tell me jokes (mostly dirty ones that are not appropriate to repeat), but boy would they make us laugh. She would laugh so hard she would start coughing and gasp for air and would have to calm herself down. After she could catch her breath I would ask her if she was ok and she would say, "Sure, who needs to breathe?" We would start laughing about that. It was very difficult to ask her anything without her turning it into something funny. I had never taken care of someone so at peace with what was happening to her and what was going to happen. She always told me that she was not afraid of dying. "What is there to be scared of?" she would always say. It wasn't just what she said; I could see in her eyes that she truly was at peace. That made me think about it and realize that there really isn't anything to be scared of, whether you are dying or not. She was always making me think and bringing out the best in me. We would always spend the first half-hour of the visit just talking and joking around, then I would do my nursing assessment and sometimes even after that we would talk some more. Our beliefs and ideas were very similar, so we always had something to talk about. I found her very interesting and loved to hear what she had to say. I only saw her once a week, per her request. She was still driving and was quite the social butterfly so she could only squeeze me in once a week, which was fine with me. Hospice encourages people to go out and do everything and anything they want for as long as they can.

No matter how hard I tried not to get close to her, she continued to pull me into her world and her heart with each visit. There was a special connection between us that cannot be explained, and I knew deep down it had a purpose. After each visit as I would walk to my car I would think to myself, "You are getting too close, you need to be more professional and less emotionally involved." But again there was something inside me saying, "There is a reason," and that feeling could not be ignored. We shared the same spiritual beliefs and would talk at length about them. It was a relief to both of us to have someone to share in the same beliefs and be able to talk about things without being looked at as "weird." She would tell me that sometimes she could feel her late husband lying next to her at night and that he would talk to her. "He is always with me, I feel his presence, and that is why I don't feel sad about him being dead."

I continued to see her weekly and saw little to no change in her condition. I couldn't wait for it to be Thursday so I could go see her. No matter what was going on with me, as soon as I saw that smile and sat down at that tiny kitchen table all my worries went away. The laughter came and everything seemed right in the world. She always brightened my day. Although she could no longer drive, she wasn't about to sit around in her house alone and feel sorry for herself. She had a group of girlfriends who would come and pick her up and they would go out to lunch and do stuff together. Iris was very aware that the time was coming when she would not be able to do much, so she was going to do everything while she still could. Sometimes she would overdo it a little bit and the next day she would tell me that she would have to rest more and that it was more difficult for her to breathe. But that did not stop her, she would just rest one day and be at it again the next day. When she wasn't out and about with her friends she was doing things around the house, cleaning things out and getting everything in order so her family would not have to do it. "I want to make sure everyone knows what they are getting and what they want because I do not want any fighting, because I will not be able to break it up."

I had been taking care of her for about three months or so when I got the idea to write this book, and just had to tell her about it. She was so excited and thought it was a great idea. She told everyone she knew about it. I would ask her advice about what to write in it, and she agreed to help me in any way she could. That's when I got the idea to follow her through her journey until the end. She agreed, but would always say, "How are you going to finish it unless you cross over with me?" I would then explain to her that the story ends with her physical death. She would just nod her head yes. "Are you sure you don't want to come with me, there is so much to do over there." I decided to pass on that proposition, and we would just smile at each other; a nervous smile because neither one of us ever wanted the story to end, but knew that someday it would. I knew that her death was going to be difficult for me but there was no turning back and I knew that it would all be worth it. I assured her that whatever happened and wherever she ended up going I was going to see her through this to the end. We made direct eye contact and she said, "Is that a threat or a promise?" I smiled and said, "Both," and her eyes lit up and she smiled at me and she said, "Good." My heart just melted.

In the middle of August she told me that she was starting to lose her appetite. "Is that part of it or am I just weird?" she asked. I told her that it was common for patients to lose their appetites. She was very aware of her body, and when something was different she wasn't afraid to ask me about it. She told me she wanted to know everything and what it meant, although once in a while she would explain an unusual pain somewhere and ask, "Is that part of the process, what does it mean?" And I would have to look at her with a blank stare while my brain was trying to find an answer. Some of her minor symptoms I had never heard of anyone else having so I would tell her, "I don't know what that means." "In other words, you are telling me I'm weird? But I already know that," she would reply, and we would start laughing. Around September and October she started slowing down physically. She said that doing anything around the house would make her breathing more difficult and she would get tired easily. She told me she had TB. I looked at her in surprise thinking that she was talking about tuberculosis, which I should have known about. She started laughing and asked me if I had ever heard of TB. And I told her the only one I knew of was the lung disease. "No," she said trying to catch her breath from laughing, "I am talking about having 'tired butt' (TB)!" It took me a minute to figure out it was a joke and then we laughed for the longest time. That was one of the funniest things she ever said.

Her breathing continued to remain stable every time I saw her, so I would sometimes find myself in denial that she was going to die. I was quickly shocked back into reality when she would have a "bad day" during one of our visits. She started having them more frequently into November. It was so difficult for me to sit there and watch her gasp for air and hear her wheezing breath from across the room. I felt so helpless because I could do nothing for her. There was silence except for the sound of her wheezing. She could not speak because of her breathing and I just didn't know what to say. We would both look at each other knowing that the worst was yet to come. She knew what lie ahead and she knew that this was a major sign that her condition was declining. Since she watched her late husband go through this she would ask me if she would die like him. I would tell her that everyone travels this journey differently and even if you suffer from the same illness doesn't mean you will have the same symptoms or die the same way. Iris took everything with such courage it made me want to cry. As the months went on I could slowly see little hints of a deteriorating condition. She never really lost much weight, the signs were her breathing and coloring in her face. She would ask me if it was "normal" to be feeling "like this." I would ask her what exactly she was feeling like and she could not describe it, just that her body felt "funny." She was surprised when I told her that it was common for patients to say they feel "funny" or "different." "Then you are saying I am not weird?" Before I could answer her she started to laugh. "You don't have to say anything, I know I'm weird." She knew what was happening, and she just needed someone to be honest with her and confirm that it was indeed a sign her condition was declining. She would always reply back with, "That's what I thought." She told me one day that she had fallen asleep in the recliner and received a message. She was very clear that it was not a dream. Iris knew that I would believe her so she felt comfortable telling me things like this. She told me that she had seen this tunnel of white light and at the end of the tunnel were four shadowy black figures and then behind them were rays of bright white light shining through. I asked her if any of them said anything. She said she heard her late husband's voice say, "It's not time yet." As soon as he said that she woke up. I asked her if there was anything scary about it and she said that everything about it was extremely peaceful. She did not know who the other three figures were. That was the only time she had that experience. Although she knew it wasn't her time yet, she wondered what she had left to do on earth. Of course, I could not answer this question for her, although she looked to me for all answers. "You are the nurse, you are supposed to know everything," she would joke. Iris continued to remain at peace and in good spirits most of the time. Occasionally she would get frustrated because she could not be as active as she used to be. "I get tired watching television," she would laugh. Since she always had a smile on her face and laughed a lot it was heartwrentching when she would have a weak moment and would start crying. The tears were that of not wanting to lose control of what was happening to her body. "I am so used to being in control of everything and this is the one thing I know I can't control and I don't like that." She would tell me that her "TB" (tired butt) was getting worse and she was having to rest and sleep more. At one visit we were talking about people dying and somehow got on the subject of the time of day people die. She jokingly said "the nerve of some of these people to die in the middle of the night, or without giving you warning." Then she said, "I promise I will give you at least two weeks notice before I die." And we both sat there and laughed for quite awhile about that one. I replied, "You better. That's the least you could do." and she continued to laugh as I said good-bye. Walking to my car I couldn't help but wonder how exactly her journey was going to end. Would it go slowly, would I really get two weeks to prepare to say good-bye, or would she quickly just slip away?

Because she lived alone she realized that the time would come for her to go to an inpatient hospice facility when her condition got too bad for her to care of herself. And she was very ok with that. While she could still drive she actually went driving around town to all the hospice facilities and "shopped" for a place to go when the time was right. She would laugh and tell me "you should have seen some of the looks I got when I walked into these places and told them I was shopping for a bed for myself." She liked to do things for shock value. She continued to want to know about what was going on in my life. Finally I would slowly open up to her and tell her little things about my life and what I had been doing but I still held so much back. No matter how bad my day was or what was on my mind I always looked forward to going to she her because I knew that she would make me laugh. The world was truly a different place when I was with her.

Into November with each visit I could see her deterioration. Her breathing was becoming much worse now. She was not just having bad periods of increased difficulty breathing anymore, now it was pretty much every time she moved. She would walk just a few feet and have to stop and catch her breath. Her breathing was extremely "wheezy" now; it sounded like an extremely severe asthma attack, sometimes even worse. I felt so helpless sitting there and watching her struggle to breathe, knowing what was happening to her and knowing there was not much I could do about it. Some days it would take her at least fifteen to twenty minutes to walk from the front door to the kitchen, which wasn't far at all. She lived in a small townhouse. She now took Roxanol (liquid Morphine) when she needed it to help ease her breathing and open up the airways in her lungs. Of course, none of this dampened her spirits and sense of humor. I would ask her how she was doing and she would say, "Great! Except for the fact that I can't breathe, but that is a minor detail, so how are you?" During our visits we would have such great conversations that sometimes I would completely forget that I was her nurse and she was in hospice dying. Yes a part of me was in denial. Well, maybe not denial but just not wanting her to die. What bothered me the most was when she would get really short of breath while talking and laughing and our conversation would have to stop. There were some days that our visits were not as long as they used to be because her shortness of breath would not allow her to talk and laugh like she used to. I could see the frustration in her eyes because she wanted to laugh and keep talking but her lungs would no longer allow that. Some visits she would just sit there and listen to me talk. I asked her one day if she felt that the time was getting closer for her to go to an inpatient facility. She nodded her head "yes," and said, "I think about it a lot, especially at night when I can't breathe and know I am alone." I asked her if she had picked a place yet. She said, "No, I am still shopping around. I know I want a private room so no one has to hear me cough and gasp around and I don't want to hear anyone doing the same." She had such an amazing attitude. She asked me how she would get there. I told her that we would call an ambulance to transport her. I said that there would be no sirens or lights, and that it would just be a transfer. "No sirens and lights?" she said, "I have always wanted to be in an ambulance with the sirens and lights." In the back of my mind I was thinking how I would convince the paramedics to give this dying woman her wish and turn on the lights and sirens. As I walked to my car, as with everytime I left her, I always thought to myself, "you are getting way too close." But for some reason I just couldn't pull away from her. I already know that her death will be difficult for me, but the friendship I got out of knowing her will be worth it.

During one of my visits Iris told me that she woke up the other night and was having chest pain. I asked her if she had had chest pain before and she said yes. I asked if she had some nitroglycerin tablets (little pills placed under the tongue, which help with chest pain). Iris told me that she had some but they were all the way downstairs. When I asked what she did, a huge grin came across her face and she said, "I did nothing. I did not want to get up and end up dying on the floor or on the stairs, if I was going to die it was going to be in my bed. She admitted that she was a little scared at first but then thought, "If it is my time, I'll go." The chest pain eventually subsided. Iris commented, "I guess it wasn't too bad because I woke up this morning." Every time I saw her she continued to amaze me with her peacefulness and humor of what she was facing. In seven years I have never come across someone quite like her. As she always said, "What can I say, I know I'm weird." By then it was getting close to Christmas and she starting asking me more questions about "feelings" she would have in her body. "What does this mean, does it mean the time is getting closer?" Of course, most of the things she described had me completely baffled, and I would just tell her I had never heard of anyone having that and I didn't know what it meant. "I wish I knew when I was going to die, I don't know whether to go Christmas shopping or not," she said and started laughing so hard she started to cough and tried to stop herself. I told her I thought she was safe and should go shopping. She then started talking about her children and grandchildren all asking her what she wanted for Christmas. In my mind I thought she would say something like, "a new pair of lungs." But Iris would not be Iris if she didn't constantly surprise me with what she said. She had one granddaughter who kept asking what she could buy her for Christmas, so Iris finally told her to buy her some sexy nightgown to wear. "Just in case I die sleeping, I want to be wearing something sexy." I asked her if that scared her granddaughter and she said that it didn't because her family was used to her comments by now. After that I felt sad because I knew that this would be her last Christmas.

The following week my visit was shorter than usual. Even though Iris's breathing was a little better than the previous week, she wasn't talking too much. Yes, we did have our usual talking and laughing before I took her blood pressure, pulse, etc., but I could tell she wanted to cut the visit short. After listening to her lungs she usually asked me how they sounded. So when asked I told her that I didn't hear much air moving in them. Of course she replied with, "Well, maybe you need to turn up your hearing aids then." This caught me off guard and it took me a few seconds to absorb it but when I did it really made me laugh. She then got more serious and told me that Bob, her deceased husband, came to "visit" her the other night. She told me that she then had an out of body experience in which she was holding Bob's hand and looking down at herself lying in her bed sleeping. Bob then said to her, "Let's go." Iris said that they went "traveling" and she remembers going around and visiting different people whom they knew that were still alive. She said she didn't remember a lot of details, and everything was like she was looking through fog, then before she knew it she was back in her bed. I am so glad she felt comfortable enough to share these stories with me. She knew that I would not think she was making them up or think she was crazy. I actually found them very fascinating and wished more of my patients would share experiences like this. Well, I could tell that she was ready for the visit to end when I asked her what she wanted to do about the next week's visit because it fell on Thanksgiving. She told me that we could just skip the visit the next week. I had to double check and asked her if she would be ok until the following week (I should have known). She came back with a quick reply of, "What is the worst that can happen? I could die? Then if that happens you won't need to worry about any visits anymore." Even though we were both laughing, there was part of me that didn't think that was funny. As I was driving home that evening I thought of her which always brings a smile to my face. "I am really going to miss her," I said to myself.

One evening after getting home from work late, I was checking my messages. I got a message from Iris, and instant panic set in. I could barely understand her, but what I could understand she said that if I had time I should come by and see her. I felt so guilty for not checking my messages sooner. I wondered if she was ok, or even still alive. Even though it was well past five o'clock if she needed me, I would have driven back out to see her, and she did not exactly live in the neighborhood. I called her and to my relief she sounded a lot better. She told me that she was just having "a bad day" and was having more frequent periods where it was very difficult to breathe. "I took some morphine, did a nebulizer treatment, sat down and thought well, if this is it, this is it." She confessed to me that she did get a little scared and really thought that was the end. I thought how eerie that would be to have that message be her last words to anyone. She said she would be ok until our regularly scheduled visit tomorrow. Words cannot say how relieved I was.

On my way to see Iris for our scheduled visit, I wasn't looking forward to it like I usually did. I guess in my heart I knew things were still not good for her physically and that her condition was declining. Unfortunately, I was right and my first clue was when she did not come to the door and let me in. The door was unlocked and she had yelled, "come in" from inside. I could barely hear her and was surprised she could even yell. I walked in and she was slumped over halfway down the hallway. She was coming to the door because she didn't think I heard her. She was grayish in color and gasping for breath. I felt so incredibly helpless and just wanted to start crying right there. This was the moment I have dreaded since I started taking care of her. Even though I knew it was coming it caught me off guard because it came faster than I thought it would. As I looked around her house, I noticed that she had decorated for Christmas and I had an instant flashback to the conversation we had just a couple weeks ago where she was joking around about whether to go Christmas shopping or not. She had slowly made her way to the kitchen chair and sat down. It took her at least thirty minutes to get to the chair, which was only about four feet from where she stood. To her it was probably more like ten miles. I didn't know what to say, so we just sat in silence for a few minutes while she tried to catch her breath. I could see her chest rising and falling with great effort for each breath, and all I heard was the sound of wheezes coming from her. All she could get out was a small whisper at this time. I knew her lungs were fighting with everything they had to keep working and could get tired out and quit at any moment. I gave her some morphine hoping that it would help. She was too weak and short of breath to do it herself.

Within fifteen minutes her breathing was a little better, enough that she could talk and the color was starting to come back into her face. She asked me what day it was and I told her, she was confused, not making much sense, which was not like her at all. She still continued to try to have a sense of humor but with the confusion it just wasn't funny that day, nothing about that day was funny. I finally had to ask her, "Do you think it is time to go into a facility?" I got no response, but I could tell she was thinking about it. "I don't know," Iris finally responded back. "Do you think you are still safe here?" She didn't know the answer to that question either. I choked down my tears because she looked so sick she didn't even look like herself and the confusion was very disturbing to me. She was always as sharp as a tack. I hate making major decisions about people's lives, but I knew that I was going to have to, and fast. She asked me for a glass of water so I went and got her one. I asked her how she had been drinking and she said that she hadn't had the strength to get herself anything to eat or drink since early yesterday morning. I offered her something to eat and she said she was not hungry. I asked her why she had not called anyone and she said that she thought that it would either pass or she would die. That was the moment that I knew it was time for her to go to a facility. I asked her one more time what she thought. She started crying and said, "I don't know, this is so hard and I thought I had a better handle on things." That about broke my heart. I was not used to seeing her cry; she always seemed so strong. Then she looked me straight in the eyes and said, "What do you think I should do? Tell me what to do." There was no getting out of this one, I knew that I had to look into her tear-filled eyes and tell her. I said in a very soft voice, "I think it's time for you to go in." She nodded her head in agreement, wiped her tears, and asked what she should bring with her. So, we started talking about making arrangements for her transfer. I called the social worker and she said she would call the facility to let them know she was coming. I asked her how she would like to get there and she said she would call her son to come and take her. There would be no lights and sirens for her. I assured her that I would meet her there. I did not want to leave her by herself but I knew that I had to. I couldn't stay there all day and had other patients who needed me, plus she jokingly kicked me out and assured me she would be fine. So, before leaving I got her settled into her recliner, turned on the television, got her some more water and a little snack in case she got hungry and made sure she had the phone right beside her. As I hesitantly closed her front door I wondered if she would just lie her head back and pass away peacefully by herself. Was this to be the last time I would ever see her? Before leaving I asked her if she had had any dreams or premonitions that the time was getting closer and she said no, which made me feel a little more comfortable leaving. She didn't believe it was her time and I believed her.

Iris did not get to the facility until late afternoon. I was exhausted from a busy day but knew I had to keep my promise. The facility was not where I envisioned her wanting to be. It was a nursing home wing so we could continue to care for her, which she thought was what she wanted at the time. I think she agreed to it because she was so familiar with the staff who had been caring for her. She just had to leave her home and did not want to lose us too. I tried to reassure her that where ever she went, whether our company was still involved in her care or not, I would be with her until the end. That was our agreement. That evening after everything that had happened that day she wanted the comfort of knowing that she was still with our hospice company, and everyone who saw her at home would come and care for her in the nursing home. The staff did not know anything about hospice care and immediately started talking about getting her into physical therapy. I knew right away this was not going to work. I felt so incredibly guilty because I was the one who finally told her that it was time to go, so she left her cozy little home and now sat in a sterile looking room with a hospital bed and all the smells and noises that filled the hallways. I made sure she got settled and got some dinner, then I went and gave the report to the nurse that was going to take care of her. She didn't understand hospice at all, no matter how much I explained it to her, which left me feeling very frustrated. The staff there was more serious than Iris was used to. Iris was feeling a little better and her sense of humor was back. The staff did not find what she said funny, and I knew that was important to her; it was a big part of who she was. I went back to reluctantly say goodbye to her, and she was in the dining room eating dinner, which was good to see. It would be hard to say when the last time was that she had eaten anything. She had a look of surprise on her face when she saw me. "What are you still doing here? Go home!" I told her that I was leaving then and that I would be back first thing in the morning. "Is that a threat or a promise?" she asked. I responded with, "Both," as a smile came across my face. She started to laugh. I still did not want to leave her. I felt like I was abandoning her. I told her if she could just make it through the night and if she didn't like it she could be moved in the morning.

First thing the next morning I was at the facility, anxious to see how her night was. I walked in her room and she was sitting on the side of her bed. She was still pretty short of breath. She didn't smile when she saw me, which was not a good sign. "Get me out of here," she said. She told me that she asked for her medications a long time before and still hadn't gotten them. "You would not believe this place!" I asked her if she wanted to go down the hall to the "hospice unit," or be transferred out to a hospice facility. She said whatever was faster. I went and called the social worker and went to talk with the staff over at the "hospice unit" down the hallway. It was staffed with the staff I used to work with from another hospice so I felt very comfortable with leaving her there. I knew they would take good care of her and they would understand her sense of humor more than the others had. The transfer happened on a Friday afternoon. Iris was told that she would no longer be with our hospice organization, but I assured her that I would still come and see her. She was fine with all of it, and relieved to get out of that other place. Monday morning seemed to be forever away before I could visit her again. At least I had peace of mind that she was in good hands with the staff over there. A lot of them were friends of mine so once they found out that Iris was my patient, she was treated like royalty.

Monday morning I found myself back at the facility talking with her in her room. She looked a lot better and her breathing was better but she looked so sad and did not have the usual sparkle in her eyes when she saw me. A part of me felt that this was my entire fault, that maybe it was too soon for her to be brought into a facility. I sat down and we talked for a while. She said that she didn't like it there and wanted to go home. She felt that her breathing was better and that she was "over the hump" and could go home. What she didn't understand was that her breathing was better because she was in a facility and people were taking care of her, and that if she went home she would have to do everything herself. "I have to try," she said, and no one could deny her that. So, I talked with the nurse and expressed her wishes and they said that they would have the social worker come and talk with her and start the transfer procedure for her to go home. It made me very sad because she was no longer with our hospice agency. When she got transferred to the facility we had to discharge her from our agency to their hospice, and because of the hospice benefit periods, she would be unable to transfer back to our hospice program for about sixty days or so. I assured her again that I would continue to come and see her, wherever she was. I got word that she did go home on Wednesday afternoon, and I planned to keep our regular Thursday morning appointment time.

Between patients I drove to her home and once again her color was grayish and her breathing was very labored. She looked just as she did before. It broke my heart because I knew how much she had hoped that she could at least stay home for a couple of days. She told me that she had been unable to do anything. "I can hardly make it to the bathroom and back and last night I peed my pants, boy was that a joy!" I just didn't even know what to say to her. She told me that there were so many things left undone in her home that only she could finish up. She once again asked me to get her a glass of water, probably the only thing she had consumed since coming home. She was getting weaker and didn't even talk or laugh as much as she did because it would make her short of breath. Her eyes started to fill with tears. "It is so hard to lose control of everything," she said. That has always been the most difficult thing for her to deal with—the loss of control. "So, what do you think I should do?" She always put the decisions back on me, which made me nervous because I was afraid I would make the wrong decision for her. "You are supposed to know everything though," she would always say. So, we talked some more and I had to be honest with her once again. I told her that I thought she needed to go back into a facility. She nodded her head yes and softly said, "Me too." I know she wished with all her heart that she would somehow get back to where she was but I knew that she was starting her decline and her disease was progressing. Her new nurse and social worker were scheduled for a visit later that afternoon and she said she would talk with them and decide then. I called the other hospice to find out who her new nurse was going to be. I wanted to make sure it was someone she could laugh with and someone who would appreciate her unique sense of humor and personality. I called one of my best friends who is a nurse over there and asked her whom she would suggest since she couldn't take her. She said one of their male nurses sounded like a good match, and he was the one who ended up being assigned to her. I felt so protective of her then and was very sad that I couldn't be her nurse. Plus, I knew how important it was for her to have someone to laugh with. When I called and started giving him a report about her I found my eyes filling with tears. I was having to let her go, in a way, before she completed her journey, and, like her, it was difficult giving up that control but I knew that I had to let the others care for her now. Her nurse called me later that same afternoon and told me that her breathing had gotten worse and she was barely able to walk around so she was transferred back into the facility. I told her before I left her house earlier that day that I would continue to follow her to the end of her journey. She smiled and said, "So, are you going to cross over with me?" I laughed and said "No, but I will be there up to that point." "Is that where your book ends, when I am dead?" I told her that after she passes away I would be ending the stories in my book. She was always so excited about my book.

When she was transferred to the hospice facility after her very short stay at home she got a different room, a room she really liked. She had all kinds of ideas of how she was going to decorate it. She knew then that this room would be her home until her death, and she was slowly coming to terms with that. It was about the second week of December. I was sad that she couldn't have at least spent her last Christmas in her own home. I kept up my weekly visits. It was always so good to see her and all my old friends who worked there. It made me feel so good to know they were caring for her. I would not have wanted her anywhere else. With constant twenty-four hour nursing care, monitoring, and medications, her breathing had finally stabilized. She still got short of breath when she exerted herself but because there were people to care for her she didn't need to exert herself much at all. She could no longer walk so she would get herself into a wheelchair and push herself around in it with her legs. "I have to keep these sexy legs in shape you know." Everyone on the staff fell in love with her immediately; it wasn't difficult to do. Her spirit just captured your heart. Physically she didn't change, some people lose a lot of weight but Iris did not. Friends and family would come and take her out to eat sometimes because she said the food there was not that great. She got a leather recliner in her room, hung up cute little curtains, and got a small bookshelf to put her stuff on. She had a bulletin board with pictures on it. She tried to make it as home-like as possible. Christmas came and went and Iris said she had a nice Christmas with her family and that Santa Claus came to visit her at the hospice and she had her picture taken with him. She always told me how amazed she was at how happy the staff was and how much laughter there was around there. Of course, she fit right in and gave the staff their fair share of laughs.

It was around New Year's Eve and of course Iris asked me what I was doing and I said, "Nothing." By then, when I said that she would just give me a look as if to say, "Get out there and live." She told me she had big plans for New Year's. She was going to go out to dinner with a good friend of hers and then she was going to come back and rest for a while. Then with a big grin on her face she showed me a beautiful cream-colored nightgown with beads and sparkles on it. It was long and flowing, and really beautiful. I imagined it being something someone would wear on their wedding night. "It's time to put this thing to some use." She told me that she was going to put that on and "stroll the hallways" looking for someone who would be worth flashing. She just started laughing and I could tell she was not kidding and was so excited about her plan. Meanwhile, I just sat there with my chin to the floor not really knowing what to think or do. Amazingly, even after all this time, she still shocked me once in a while.

The following week she told me that she did wear the nightgown but did not find anyone worthy of flashing. We both laughed at that. Iris knew everything that was going on there. She knew who was who and the families and patients and when someone died. I asked her if it bothered her that people were constantly dying around her. "No," she replied. "We are all going to die." Iris told me that she admired anyone who did hospice work. "It must be so difficult for you guys to be losing your patients all the time." The smoking area was right outside her bedroom window and she told me one day she heard someone crying out there, so she got herself into her wheelchair and wheeled herself out there to find one of the staff members crying because they had just lost a patient they had grown fond of (it happens to all of us). Iris ended up consoling and supporting that staff member the best she could. "You guys need support too," she told me. Not only did Iris have an amazing sense of humor but also an amazing heart. She would also console patients' family members whom she would get to know. Her room had an open door for anyone who needed a shoulder to cry on or someone to listen. I was in awe of her doing all of this and told her how wonderful I thought it all was. Of course, she brushed it off like it was nothing, "They all just need someone to just listen, they need to talk their pain out, and I am here for that. I would much rather be making a difference than lying in my room waiting to die."

Iris always thought of everyone else's happiness first. One of my good friends was working that day and we started talking about a party that the hospice was having where everyone got dressed up and went out for dinner and dancing. Iris looked at me and asked me if I was going. I explained to her that I couldn't go because I no longer worked for this hospice and the party was just for the employees. "You have to find a way to go," she said. "You need to crash that party somehow." When any staff person who would stop in her room to say "Hi, Iris," she would ask them if they knew of a way for me to go to the party. I will never quite understand why it was so important to her that I go; it was just a party. After everyone stopped dropping by her room we started to have our usual visit. It was a good visit. She looked good and her breathing was under control, although she did tell me that she could feel "inside" that she was getting worse. "All part of the process right?" she would say, as if talking about the weather or something. Iris said that she never envisioned a hospice facility to be so nice to be in. "It has far exceeded my expectations and imagination." I asked her if she missed her home and she said, "No, not really." Her response surprised me but made me feel very content knowing she liked where she was so well. Iris said that she felt so safe there knowing that a nurse was always right there if she needed something. She said she slept better knowing she was not alone. The day before my visit she got into the whirlpool bath they have there and a volunteer came and gave her a massage. Almost every afternoon the cocktail cart would come by and she would have a glass of wine. During my visit the cocktail cart did come so she got a glass of wine and some chips. A little later a volunteer came by with her beagle dog for pet therapy. Iris liked dogs, so the dog was "visiting" for awhile. "Who knew that waiting to die would be such a luxury?" she would laugh and joke about. All the staff is so nice and just right there when you need them. "I have no regrets, she said. "Now I know it was the right time to come here when I did." I cannot explain how good that made me feel. For so long in the back of my mind I was always wondering if I made the wrong decision for her, now I knew I did the right thing. She told me that she had seen a couple of patients get pretty confused before they died and that bothered her. "The only thing that scares me is that I do not want to get confused, and if I do that is the point I want to be kept sedated so I don't know what is going on. The minute I lose control of my mind and/or my body I want out of here," she told me. And for once, she was not joking around. We finished up our visit and I left. My heart ached a little that day because we had such a good visit and I did not want it to end. I was also scared for her, knowing that she did not want to be confused and linger. I wished I could see into the future to see how she would die; I guess more to prepare myself for it than anything else. Even though I knew that losing her was going to hurt, I never once thought of just walking away. For the first time in my life I found myself not running away from something I knew would hurt in the end. We were destined to meet one another and to teach each other lessons—lessons on living and dying. There were lessons on laughter, and facing fears.

The big party was less than a week away and Iris was asking everyone if they knew of a way that I could go to the party. It was somehow her mission to see that I ended up at that party. It wasn't that I didn't want to go, but if I didn't that was fine too. I waited for someone to cancel, then I could go in their place, but days went by and nothing. I thought about just showing up after the dinner. I knew no one would care, but the day of the party I still had heard nothing so I decided that I was just going to stay home. Around three o'clock in the afternoon my friend called me and said that he was feeling sick and was not going to go and he needed me to go in his place so he would not get charged. So, I dressed up and went to the party and had a wonderful time. It was so good to see all my old co-workers. I took lots of pictures and was so excited to show them to Iris. I had made the dress I wore, and was very proud of it, so I had my friend's husband take a picture of just me. Iris would be so excited and proud. The following workweek was so busy that I had, for the first time, not made my weekly visit to Iris. I don't know what kept me that busy and I know now there is no excuse. She was doing so well our last visit and I wanted to wait until I had a chance to develop the pictures from the party to visit her. No one had called me to say she wasn't doing well so I had planned to visit her the next Tuesday after work. That weekend I came up with some more questions that I wanted her to answer for the book. It seemed like there was so much more I wanted her to tell me about what she was going through.

Tuesday came and it was a bitterly cold day in early February. I started seeing my patients early because I wanted to get done so I could go see Iris. We had such a good visit last time and I was hoping for another nice visit. I was excited to see her and show her the pictures from the party and tell her all about it. I was also looking forward to asking her some more questions and was always curious as to her responses. There was so much more I wanted to learn from her. So, after work I hurried over to the hospice facility with pictures and my list of questions in hand. I hurried through the hallways of the facility, picturing the smile on her face as she looked at the pictures and found out that I had made it to the party. I always stopped at the nurses' station first to say hi to everyone. A friend of mine happened to be her nurse. He immediately told me that she was not doing well. He has been known to joke around a lot, so I remember saying, "You're joking, right?" He said, "No, I'm not." I knew that he was not joking by the look on his face. I just stood there thinking, "How can this be?" I fought back tears and asked about her condition and when it started. The nurses said she had been up making coffee for the staff on Sunday, and was all right the day after and was a little more short of breath but still wheeling herself around in the wheelchair. During the early morning hours she had wet the bed so they put a Foley catheter in her bladder. She was a little weaker and a little confused but still wanted to go out and smoke. The staff had to help her into the wheelchair and back into bed. She got back into bed around one o'clock and I arrived around three. I asked them if she was awake and they both shook their heads no. Still, as I gathered the strength to go see her, a part of me was saying, "Nah, she can't be as bad as they say." I marched right into her room with no fear, not even pausing, wanting to prove them wrong, or maybe it was to prove myself wrong, but it was all true. As soon as I hit the inside of her room I stopped instantly and just stared at her. She was lying on her back in her bed with her eyes closed, oxygen on, and Foley bag hanging on the side of the bed. "She must hate that," I thought to myself. Her breathing was very labored and she was having periods when she would not breathe for fifteen to twenty seconds (apnea), and with each breath I wondered if it would be her last. Once in a while she would take a big, deep breath, but the rest of the time she was fighting for every breath. I tiptoed over and sat down next to her bed. Surprisingly, I didn't know what to say nor do, being a hospice nurse you think I would know. I put the pictures and list of questions on the floor, knowing she would never see the pictures or be able to answer the questions. I started gently stroking her arm and found myself saying, "Oh Iris," over and over. I took her limp hand in mine, it was still warm but purplish in color. I finally told her with a shaking voice I was there and she opened her eyes only for a brief moment. She kept trying to talk but could only mumble stuff I did not understand. I just sat there not believing this day was here, and wondering how this all happened so fast. Her face looked peaceful, and I asked her if she was uncomfortable and she mumbled, "no." The longer I sat there the more difficult it became to hold back my tears, and I'm not sure why I was trying to anyway. I kept waiting for her to open her eyes and talk to me. I was waiting for something funny to come from her mouth, but being a hospice nurse I knew better. At that moment I didn't feel like a hospice nurse, I felt like a normal, everyday human being losing someone I had come to care about. The tears came and went; I tried my best to catch them all in a Kleenex but noticed some of them dropped down onto her arm and I wondered if she could feel them. I wondered if she knew I was crying. I asked her to squeeze my hand, and she said, "Ok," but there was no squeeze. I sat there for a while longer trying to talk to her as if she was awake, but I found that to be very difficult because I really didn't know what to say, and I found that the more I tried to talk to her the more my heart hurt and the more I cried because I knew the end of her journey was soon, and I was not ready, but are you ever ready? I told her that I brought pictures from the party and that she had her room fixed up really nice. I don't exactly know how long I sat there but after a while I knew that I had to say my last good-bye and leave. I asked her if Bob, her late husband, was there to get her. She said, "No, he will be here later." Some things she said very clearly. I told her that I was going to go and I asked her if it was time for her to go and she said yes. I told her that she and Bob would be together again soon and she got the biggest smile on her face and mumbled a weak yes. I am going to miss that toothless, beautiful smile.

It took me a while to actually get up and walk away. It was difficult to leave her knowing that this was it, the end of our journey together. I said good-bye one more time and she opened her eyes for a brief moment and very clearly said, "I feel really good about this, it's ok." She repeated this statement at least three times and each time it was very clear. Then she closed her eyes and very clearly said to me, "Now go home and be good, love." I knew in my heart that those would be the last words she would say to me, and actually those were her last words before she became unresponsive. I knew that it was her way of telling me that I had sat there and cried over her long enough, and now I needed to go on with life. It was so hard for me to get up from that chair, turn my back to her, and walk out. I finally did leave her room but stood in the doorway just watching her for a while, not quite ready to walk away. As I watched her struggle to breathe a part of me was hoping it would all be over for her soon. She always told me she did not want to linger and as soon as she started becoming confused she wanted to be kept sedated and wanted to die sleeping peacefully. The staff was honoring her wishes. She was getting medicated every two hours to keep her comfortable and sedated. I told my friend to call me with any changes or at the time of her death.

I walked to my car feeling numb, and as I walked through the hallway of the busy nursing home it was quiet. I wondered if people could tell that I was upset, and if they could, if they would care. Once I was in my car I finally felt like I could let go and I just sat there and cried. I don't know how long, but I remember having the window down a little bit and feeling the frigid cold on my face. I was looking up at the cloudy sky and could see the sun all covered with clouds. It was eerie. Then a peaceful feeling came over me and I thought to myself, "Why are you crying? She was not afraid, she is ready and would not want you to be out here crying." There was part of me that still found it very difficult to believe that I would never see her smile light up a room, and never get to laugh with her again. A part of me regrets not going to see her the previous week and putting off some of the things I wanted to ask her and talk with her about. Now those answers will go with her. I was surprised that when I got home I did not cry anymore. I didn't feel the need to. I had a feeling deep inside me that I cannot describe, but somehow I knew that everything would be all right and that she would always be with me. The phone did not ring that night. I went to sleep thinking of her and couldn't help but smile. What a wonderful person. I woke up and saw that no one had called during the night. I called the facility to check on Iris and a friend of mine answered the phone and said that she was just getting ready to call me, and that Iris had passed away around seven o'clock in the morning with her son by her bedside. She said that Iris passed away peacefully in her sleep, just as she had wanted. Even though I am sad, every time I think of her a smile comes across my face and I feel very privileged to have known her and for her to allow me to come along on this journey with her. I am glad I got to say good-bye to her and that she knew that I was there and that I kept my promise of seeing her through this to the end.

The day I learned of her death it was difficult to get myself together and go to work, but I knew I had to. Iris no longer needed me, but my patients and their families still needed me and counted on me. I actually held it together better than I thought I could. There were periods during the day when I would think of her being gone and my eyes would fill with tears. Then I would hear her in my head saying, "There is no reason to be sad, for I am still with you, stay strong." I know that she helped give me the courage and strength to get through the first few days following her death. I feel her with me every day, and as long as I have that feeling I am not sad. I know that she will watch over me and give me the strength I need to go through life. She taught me about living life, and I know she is always going to be pushing me to, "Go out there and have fun." Even though she is no longer here physically, she taught me that we can still continue relationships with those who go before us. The relationship just has to change. She left me with peace of mind and her strength, and I will always remember, "There is no reason to ever be afraid."

Iris truly opened my eyes to life. She taught me that it is possible to keep your spirits up and keep living your life even though you have a terminal illness. She taught me that you can find humor in any situation if you choose to see it. According to her, that was the way to go. "Laugh a lot, life is funny!" she would say. Iris made me realize that we all need to go out have fun, worry less, and not be afraid. She always thought society, as a whole was way too serious. Love and make friendships wherever you can, she believed. Care for strangers just because they are humans and they feel pain too. We need to take the time to care for others no matter what you yourself are going through. There is always room in your life for caring and laughter. These were things she taught me. Iris was dying, and yet she always found the time to make others laugh or comfort those who had just lost someone they love. Never once did she think of her own illness or death. She was never scared that she might be next. She was too busy giving 100% to those she felt needed comfort and caring (which was everyone she encountered). Iris would always tell me to take chances, and that I have nothing to lose but would always gain the wisdom of knowing that I took a chance and tried. She always would remind me, "Live with no regrets, and do not fear death."

I was not sad that I was not there to see her take her last breath. That was a private time for her and her family, and if she wanted me there she would have made sure I was there. She did allow me to say good-bye and wanted to talk with me one last time and I feel very privileged to have known her and for her to allow me to follow her on her journey.

I wrote the poem "Don't Cry" a couple of days after her death. I wrote it to help me through a difficult time and what I believe it says what she would tell me if she could.

# *Don't Cry*

Don't cry for me
For I am ok
And I am exactly where I am supposed to be
In the arms of my love once again

It was time for me to leave my diseased body behind
It was starting to smother who I was
And it had served its purpose
I did everything I was sent here to do
It was time for my soul to travel on
And I have so much work to do on the other side

Do not be afraid
There is never any reason to be afraid
And if you ever find yourself feeling scared
Draw courage and strength from my guidance
And remember you are never alone

Do not mourn the loss of me
But celebrate my life
For it was filled with laughter and love
Remember me with a smile
Not tears

Know that I will be celebrating my freedom
Freedom from sickness and pain
I am at peace now
And I wish for you to be at peace with me

Do not cry for me
For I am not really gone

I will be watching over you
So be good
And continue to talk to me
Because I will be listening
Continue to laugh
And know I will be laughing with you

In times of loneliness, uncertainty
And pain
Just think of me
I will be the one wiping away your tears
Giving you the strength to make it through
And spreading my angel wings around you
To hold you tight in comfort and in love

Do not cry for me
There is no need for tears
Or sadness
For death is not the end
But it is the beginning of a beautiful new adventure
And I will remain full of life even in death

# *About the Author*

Erin is a native of Colorado. She currently lives in Denver, and continues to be a home hospice nurse. She received her Bachelor's Degree in Nursing from Regis University. You may contact her at elmrn@msn.com.

# Recommended Readings

*Life Lessons* by Elizabeth Kubler-Ross, David Kessler

*Tuesdays With Morrie* by Mitch Albom

*On Death and Dying* by Elizabeth Kubler-Ross

*Final Gifts* by Maggie Callanan, Patricia Kelly

*The Cocktail Cart* by Edward Bear

*How We Die* by Sherwin B. Nuland

*The Five People You Meet in Heaven* by Mitch Albom

*Dying Well* by Ira Byock

*Caregiving: Hospice proven techniques for the healing of body and soul* by Douglas C. Smith, Doug Smith

*Handbook of Hospice Care* by Robert W. Buckingham

*For the Living: Coping, Caring, and Communicating with the Terminally Ill* by Mark Golubow

*Lessons from the Dying* by Rodney Smith, Joseph Goldstein

You may also contact your local or state hospice organizations

0-595-31464-3

Printed in the United States
22478LVS00006B/276

9 780595 314645